1990

PHOTOGRAPHER'S DIALOGUE

Popular and Preferred Imagery in American Photography

By

Steven Carothers

and

Gail Roberts

Introduction By A.D. Coleman

Published By

SIRS

and

Boca Raton Museum of Art

Published by Social Issues Resources Series, Inc. (SIRS)

P.O. Box 2348, Boca Raton, Florida 33427

ISBN 0-89777-127-3

Library of Congress Cataloging-in-Publication Data

Carothers, Steven, 1954-
Photographer's dialogue : popular and preferred imagery in American photography / by Steven Carothers. Gail Roberts; introduction by A.D. Coleman.
p. 144 cm. 28
ISBN 0-89777-127-3
1. Photography, Artistic—Exhibitions. I. Roberts, Gail, 1947-. II Title.
TR645.B63B6323 1989 89-27794
779'.0973'07475932—dc20 CIP

Book Design by: Steven Carothers

Printed in U.S.A.

CONTENTS

Acknowledgements 4

Director's Statement 5
Roger L. Selby

Foreword 7
Steven Carothers and Gail Roberts

Expression and Communication 9
An Essay By A.D. Coleman

Elements Of Acceptance 15
Steven Carothers and Gail Roberts

Popular and Preferred 43
The Images

The Photographers 104
Statements and Biographies

Bibliography and Credits 139

ACKNOWLEDGMENTS:

Organizing the exhibit and publishing this catalogue involved the cooperation and assistance of many people. We wish to thank Roger L. Selby, Director, for giving us the opportunity to complete a project of this magnitude. Our thanks to Eleanor and Elliot Goldstein, of SIRS, for publishing this book in coordination with the museum and for their generous support. Many of the artists involved in the project were located with the help of Arthur and Fatima NeJame of the Palm Beach Photographic Workshops; their dedication to bringing quality photography to South Florida is appreciated by all of us. A special thanks to John Mayer, of South Florida Art Services, for his generous donation of time and labor in framing the sixty photographs for the exhibit. Our appreciation goes to A.D. Coleman for his insightful introduction, to the Boca Museum staff, and to the numerous galleries and institutions, whose cooperation enabled us to assemble the necessary information and required photographs. Finally, our most sincere thanks to the featured artists in this project; their responses to our questions, and patience in answering our numerous correspondence, provided us with a greater understanding of the nature of popular and preferred imagery.

Steven Carothers & Gail Roberts
Curators

This Exhibition was sponsored by:

and

MFMJ

MOORE, FARMER, MENKHAUS & JURAN, P.A.
ATTORNEYS AT LAW

Partial funding for this catalogue provided by:

DIRECTOR'S STATEMENT:

The museum takes great pride in presenting this exhibit and catalogue. It is indeed an ambitious project for a facility and staff of our size. However our strong and continued interest in photography provided the necessary incentive.

My sincere appreciation to Steven Carothers and Gail Roberts for successfully completing this project; to Fatima and Arthur NeJame who through The Palm Beach Photographic Workshops provided us the initial access to the photographers; to our museum friends Eleanor and Elliot Goldstein of SIRS without whom we would not have been able to publish this catalogue; to Beaumont Newhall with whom I had the pleasure of studying and who remains a guiding inspiration to anyone interested in the history of photography; and finally to the thirty photographers without whose cooperation this exhibition would not have been possible.

Roger L. Selby
Executive Director

FOREWORD:

From 1986 through 1989 the Boca Museum presented a photography lecture series in cooperation with Arthur and Fatima NeJame, directors of the Palm Beach Photographic Workshops. As a result of this program, the Museum's director, Roger L. Selby, introduced the idea of creating an exhibit presenting the artwork of lecturing artists visiting Boca Raton. The idea evolved into the concept of having selected photographers provide their most popular image as well as their own personal favorite. The exhibit promised to be relatively straightforward to organize. We were curious as to whether a comparison between the well-known image and the preferred image might in some way give insight into the question of why a particular image by a photographer becomes widely accepted, while other images do not receive the same attention and recognition.

The idea seemed direct enough; select approximately thirty photographers and have each provide their most popular and preferred images, an artist's statement regarding the selected artwork, a biography and finally, a picture of themselves. Discussion followed as to which photographers to invite, and what images would be considered most popular. It is here that the surprises began, and our well planned project took on a life of it's own.

Locating and making contact with the artists was one of the very first difficulties encountered. By using old catalogs, an outdated copy of Photographic Artists and Innovators, and contacts at various galleries, we were slowly able to proceed.

Upon discussing the idea with several artists, we quickly realized that some type of definition for the terms "popular" and "preferred" had to be established. In addition, it was apparent that photographers do not appreciate having their images regarded as "popular." Serious photographers tend to be apprehensive about having their creations indiscriminately grouped with images which are embraced by the masses. Armed with this new information, we set out to clarify and explore.

Steven Carothers and Gail Roberts

EXPRESSION AND COMMUNICATION

What makes a photograph *matter* in this culture? Why, that is, do we not only favor certain pictures as individual viewers, but sometimes respond to them similarly, collectively, in such numbers that the constellated reaction becomes an index of some cultural resonance between image and audience? Futhermore, what makes a photograph important to its maker, what makes it important to the public, and what relation — if any — pertains between these two affinities?

These fascinating questions, and more are raised by this exhibition. Its premise is quite simple: some thirty photographers have been asked to identify both their most "popular" image (based on concrete evidence, such as frequency of publication or volume of print sales) and their "preferential" image or personal favorite, as well as to present some statement concerning the two.

That the results provide no clear-cut answers is only to be expected. Could we have hoped for some formula that would clarify all, a recipe — say, that for an image to catch the public eye requires representation of the breast of a woman between the ages of seventeen and thirty-three, half of any tree-grown fruit, two highlights, and a depth of field of no less than twenty inches? Or that, in order to remain engaging to its maker, it must either contain three obscure autobiographical referents or else involve the solution of some arcane technical dilemma?

This show offers no such prescription. Rather than mistaking it for a search for the solution to some problem, let us take it for what it really is: an occasion for meditation of the subject of the difference between self-expression and communication.

Self-expression is an act or function whose effectiveness has only one judge — the person doing the expressing. It's my opinion that the statement "You're not expressing yourself well" is semantic nonsense. (If a relative dies and I opt to manifest my response by (a) wearing black for a year, (b) throwing a party and tying one on, or (c) going about as if nothing had happened, no one but I can tell whether I've expressed my reaction effectively.)

Self-expression, then, is fundamentally solipsistic; intentionally, it serves no one but the person doing the expressing. For that reason, it is the primary concern of only those artists who work "for themselves" — that is, those who are thereby self-defined as amateurs. The professional artist begins with self-expression, but is concerned with something beyond that: communication.

That commitment to communication involves acknowledging the existence of the Other — embodied in the audience, whether actual or hypothetical, identifiable or imagined. This acknowledgement is signalled by accepting the imperative of a shared symbol system, which is the first requisite of communicative activity. (If I wish to convey to some Other that my relative's passing has caused me grief, I'd best employ the cultural rituals of mourning; drunken revels, however much they might salve my wounds, are not widely equated with tears.)

This does not mean that all communications must be reduced to the literal or simplistic; states of mind and feeling are among the transmissions we receive from artists. Nor does it mandate any artist's uncritical adoption of some extant symbol system lock, stock and barrel; one of the functions of professional artistic activity is the generation of new symbols and the redefinition of older ones. But it does imply that the professional artist is producing not mnemonics for him/herself but communications, *messages* — intended to be received, open to interpretation, and subject to evaluation.

Unlike self-expression, the effectiveness of communication can be judged. If the audience laughs at the object with which you sought to make them gasp in fright, you the maker have failed to manipulate the symbolic structure effectively so as to evoke the psychoids of fear. The audience thus serves the artist not only as a target for the communication but as a tool for refining its delivery. When an artist pays attention to it, the audience's response to his or her work functions as what Norbert Weiner first defined as the "feedback loop," enabling the artist to use past performance to improve future performance. Certainly one of the useful functions criticism can provide to the artist is its service as feedback, as *information* — as a gauge of the differences between the message sent and the message received.

Although many of those represented in this show clearly care about the viewers' reactions to their works, none of these photographers appear to have the foggiest notion of what makes their most popular image popular. Wisely, even when they describe the favorable reception of these images few of them attempt to *explain* it, perhaps realizing that the only way to uncover the cause of that acceptance would be to interrogate the receivers, the audience, ourselves. (This could be done; perhaps someone has already attempted such an experiment. The utterances of all those who've commented publicly on a particular work could be scanned and correlated for recurrent mentions of particular aspects, similarities of interpretation, and such. Polls could be taken of museum-goers, interviews recorded with owners of prints. Perhaps we would learn something of value by this.)

In some cases, of course, we can point to obvious reasons for the appeal of a picture. Elliott Erwitt's rendition of the 1959 "kitchen debate" between U.S. Vice-President Richard Nixon and Soviet Chairman Nikita Khrushchev is an image of two major world figures on an occasion of confrontation in which the American protagonist towers over his seemingly chastened opponent and is aggressing on him; small wonder Americans love it. (In the Soviet Union it is hardly so popular.)

Similarly, Arnold Newman's portrait of Picasso is an intense, transactional portrait, made at intimate distance, of the twentieth-century artist who, more than any other, embodies "modern art" for the western world. In such cases, without denying the craft skills that went into the pictures' making, it is sensible to assert that the literal subject matter dominates the viewer's response; remove the identities of Nixon, Khrushchev and Picasso and you can be sure these images would not be anywhere near so celebrated.

Sometimes, too, the decisions of "gatekeepers" — historians, critics, curators, gallery owners, editors, publishers — assure an image's "popularity." Photographs chosen, perhaps by a single individual, to be widely reproduced for commercial purpose (as posters or postcards, for instance) can become "popular" simply because they're more effectively disseminated and readily available than others. What appears on the cover of a magazine — Joyce Tenneson's ***Suzanne*** for example, twice used in such fashion — may be determined by a lone editor's notion of the demographics of the periodical's readership.

The image selected to stand as emblematic of an artist's larger body of work on the dust jacket of a monograph or the announcement of an exhibition, the one sent out to accompany the press release for either, may be picked for all kinds of reasons, including the mundane one that it promises to reproduce more easily than another that is otherwise no less "good." So, too, the picture utilized by a historian to represent a photographer's output in a survey of the medium may be the only one in his or her institution's collection. In all of these cases, massive distribution virtually guarantees recognizability, which is often equated with (and, indeed, sometimes becomes) popularity.

Another issue is, of course, timing. Mary Ellen Mark's unflinching portrait of *Tiny,* a teen-age prostitute, appeared just as public awareness of the scope of the runaway-teen problem was developing. The nude portraits of young girls by Sally Mann, Sheila Metzner and Bea Nettles were made in a period when the advances of certain forms of feminism had surmounted puritanical hostility to the female body and denial of the sexuality of children. Twenty years ago they might not have been exhibitable — and may not be again, twenty years hence. And how else but in terms of timing are we to explain the fact that the germinal photomontages of Val Telberg, who has been working in essentially the same style for half a century, are just now achieving the recognition in photography and art circles that they've enjoyed for decades among the cognoscenti of experimental literature? Some conjunction of the work and the historical moment is clearly connected to popularity.

It seems to me that the truest gauges of popularity — of a genuine *vox populi* response — would be frequency of sales in either original print or poster form, and the kind of imitation that George Tice speaks of so fondly in regard to his ***Two Amish Boys,*** whereby the image becomes a cultural icon to such an extent that versions of its basic form appear in other media. (Something similar happened to Dorothea Lange's ***Migrant Mother:*** it has been variously converted to needlepoint, hand-drawn, silkscreened onto velvet; its protagonists have been transformed into Asians, Hispanics, and Blacks. Now that's popularity!)

So this exhibit gives us the chance to examine a group of photographs that, by no conscious, deliberate plan of their makers, somehow caught the imagination of the general audience — along with a parallel set of works that have sustained their makers' attention and affection. I suspect there is a pattern to be identified that might weave each group together. But I'm convinced we will not be the ones to find it — at least not yet, for most of these pictures are too recent for us to have any long view of them as symptoms of the zeitgeist. The oldest of them — Edward Weston's ***Pepper No. 30*** — was made fifty-eight years ago, yet it is only within the past decade that we've become able to analyze its impact on our cultural way of seeing. Surely it will take at least that much time for us to discover what linked these more recent images to our collective unconscious. In conclusion, then, we may find ourselves at exhibit's end no closer to answering the questions underlying this exhibit than we were when we entered it. But that does not mean our time has been ill spent. Far from it. What we have done is draw nearer to the actualization of our critical capacities as viewers. For, as we so commonly aver, you can't argue with taste; nothing closes off a discussion of a work of art so completely as the assertion, "I like it."

Criticism, on the other hand, is for arguing with — and one of the main stimuli for some of our most heated arguments is the curious fact that many images important to us do not appeal to our "taste." So criticism can be said to begin at the point where we set aside or move beyond our simplest response patterns, unsatisfied with mere declarations of taste, to ask ourselves that more provocative question: *Why?*

A.D. Coleman

Staten Island, New York

November 1988.

ELEMENTS OF ACCEPTANCE

ELEMENTS OF ACCEPTANCE:

Our investigation began with an attempt to identify a popular image. The term **Popular** encompasses a large segment of photographic images, generally consisting of those which are pleasing, and enjoyed by the masses. They are familiar, easy to comprehend and suitable to a wide audience. A popular photograph might be exemplified by the image of Buzz Aldrin and the American flag on the moon. It was taken by Neil Armstrong during the first United States lunar walk, and has been reproduced internationally for advertising, publication, and television. Even lunch boxes for children have been decorated with this photograph. The reason behind the popularity of this image is that it transmits multiple messages, all of which are relatively easy for the public to grasp. The image carries political overtones and celebrates the triumphs of science and American technology. It also symbolizes patriotism along with a majestic accomplishment of humankind. An image such as this often crosses barriers of age, culture and education.

What constituted a popular image for this exhibit? Each photographer was asked to submit the image which he/she felt had received the widest attention as evidenced by frequency of publication, number of sales, most often requested for exhibition or other criteria equally justifiable. This selection process is not easily accomplished. Most artists do not keep precise records of such information, and if available, each detail must be judged for significance. One photograph might have been reproduced more often, while another may have been the most collected. We found we could not base our request on any one criterion, since not one seemed to apply to all photographers. As an example, basing popularity on recognizability is not effective in finding the most popular work of Arnold Newman because many of his images fit into this category. His print of Igor Stravinsky at the piano is certainly one of his better known images; it has been widely exhibited and reproduced. However, portraits of Pablo Picasso, Georgia O'Keefe, Piet Mondrian, or Alfred Krupp are all highly recognizable and identifiable with Newman. Perhaps these images would be better described as signature images. They are readily attributable to the photographer, and most often represent a specific body of work, distinguished by the artist's characteristic style.

Many images that become popular fall well outside of the artist's main body of work. An example of this might be Judy Dater's ***Imogen and Twinka at Yosemite.*** This image was taken at a photography workshop. Though the image is well composed and handled with the same skill as other work by Dater, anyone familiar with her style would probably not attribute this work to her. Perhaps it is because the photograph was taken with a less serious purpose in mind. As she states, "My original intent, however, was simple, to make a nice snapshot of these two people for myself, and as a class demonstration."[1] So we can see that although this image is immensely popular it is certainly not a signature image.

When we discussed the concept of popular imagery with various people in the art community a frequent response was, "Popular? Oh, you mean superficial!" To some degree this is understandable, for if the intent of this exhibit was simply to establish what makes an image "popular," in a broad and general sense of the term, we need not have gone to the trouble of contacting these artists. We simply could have gone to the nearest shopping mall, picked up an image of a flower, or a woman in a bikini, and asked people what they thought. Answers such as: "that's nice," "it's pretty," or "it's exciting," could have confirmed the fact that the masses are attracted to images that tend to be superficial. This is one reason why artists, although desirous of acceptance, are cautious about the way in which the public is introduced to their photographs.

In order to complete our comparison, we petitioned the artists for an image that either characterized their artistic intent or one that held personal meaning. These images were designated as **Preferred**. Choosing this personal favorite was the most difficult task for many of the artists. When we first asked Paul Caponigro to submit his favorite image, he referred to his photographs as "children," stating that all his images were of equal importance. Many artists expressed a similar regard for their artwork; each image had its own special merits. Most artists were apprehensive about declaring one work as favorite. Therefore, it should be noted that each image in this catagory is simply one of perhaps many favorites.

The specific reasons behind the selection of each image chosen as preferred were as varied as the images themselves. Upon inspection, several broad catagories began to emerge. Some images represented pleasurable experiences or personal moments which still contained a certain intensity of feeling or sentimentality. Other images were chosen because they represented a type of turning point in the photographer's artistic philosophy or personal ambition. Judy Dater stated, ***"My Hands, Death Valley,*** . . . marked a breakthrough or revelation about a new direction for me in my life and work."[2]

Many photographers explained that the preferred image held a type of symbolic importance for them, representing issues or concerns of the artist. Regarding her favorite, Mary Ellen Mark said, "This is one of my favorite photographs because I believe it successfully shows how I felt about the Damm family; their loneliness, their desperation. I also hope that this family can stand as a symbol about how it feels to be homeless in America."[3]

Effective representation of artistic goals, and enduring interest or personal philosophy were among the most common and important criteria used in the selection process. To Duane Michals, ***Illuminated Man,*** "illustrates my idea of enlightenment."[4] About his image ***Priest,*** Ralph Gibson remarked, "it positions me aesthetically exactly where I want to be." [5] As Jerry Uelsmann stated, "While I have many favorites, the untitled image of the rope floating over the table has sustained it's mystery for me over many years. I find it to be both engaging and enigmatic."[6]

After reading the artists' statements, we began to see a similarity between the categories of Popular and Preferred. The key issue seemed to be *acceptance.* What makes one image more acceptable to an individual over another? Therefore, at this point, we ask the reader/viewer to leave behind the terms Popular and Preferred and investigate with us the factors that influence acceptance.

There are many components which affect the degree of acceptance an image might receive such as appeal, visibility, accessibility and relevancy. Though the ultimate effect of these elements is often beyond the artist's control, the potential success of an image is dependent on how well they are utilized. Among these, one of the primary issues is appeal. How appealing is the subject matter and does it hold the viewer's interest long enough for other factors to come into play?

In some situations we can more readily find clues as to why an image might have far-reaching public appeal. In Tom McCartney's ***Mount McKinley, Alaska,*** 1982, we are confronted with the magnificence of nature. This image instantly conveys the power and scale of the mountain in the landscape. The tonal range is broad and the clarity and texture of the landscape are effectively represented. The subject matter's inherent beauty tends to be universally appealing, and most often generates widespread acceptance.

In many photographs, we are likely to find that the image provides a pleasurable or fascinating experience for the viewer. This is essential whether the experience is one of excitement, serenity, beauty, sensuality, or even the intellectual, innovative or perverse qualities an image might convey. The better an image can attract, interest, amuse, or stimulate the mind and/or emotions, the greater its ability to maintain viewer interest.

While the enduring ability of an image is largely dependent on subject matter and composition, the vehicle of exposure is extremely important. The more frequently an image is seen and the larger the audience, the better the possibility of image acceptance. One of the greatest vehicles for visibility is publication. The photographers seem to agree that image demand is in some way affected by publication, but to what extent no one could say. Many photographers do exercise some control over when or where their images are reproduced, although the final decision generally resides with the publication's editor or designer.

Publishers may choose an image for any number of reasons. It may be important and representative of the artist's work. It might be the right color, shape or size for the publication, or it may be the only image available. The artwork chosen may not be the best image; it may not be their favorite. Regarding her choice for preferred, ***Three Women, Two Men, One Child,*** Joyce Tenneson states, "One editor said she loved it, but wouldn't reproduce it because it reminded her of a concentration camp scene."[7]

In an attempt to get an image and themselves known via the media, some photographers do take an active role in the conscious reproduction of certain images for the purpose of increased recognition and visibility. They produce postcards, posters and books, or they allow the work to be published in magazines. This is one area where photography excels over other artistic mediums. According to Ralph Gibson, "one of the reasons I do so many books, is that photography gives good reproduction."[8]

It would seem that there is no better way of quickly getting an image known than by mass media. But this method does have an element of risk; much of its success depends greatly on the type of publication, timing and audience. If photographers were only interested in high visiblity, the location and frequency of publication would be of little consequence. But mass media can become an enemy and quickly destroy the acceptance an artist is trying to cultivate. As Ralph Gibson states, "When you have a well known or famous photograph, the question is — how did you keep it pure? How did you manage to survive the media? Because there is one law in photography, the bigger the audience, the lower the content. So when I fool around with mass media, I'm very,

very careful. I want mass media, but I want it to work in a positive way."[9]

Another important feature of publication that directly affects acceptance is credibility. When an image is reproduced on the cover of a magazine or a book, it lends a note of importance to the image. If the book happens to be a monograph of an artist's body of work, so much the better. General reaction is often positive. If the publication is a catalogue from the Museum of Modern Art, it receives an instant seal of approval. The work has been elevated in significance and position through its institutional affiliation. If it appears on the cover of an auction catalogue an aura of value may be attributed to it.

When dealing with a specific image, of a nude for example, our perception of the importance of the image and the caliber of the photographer is greatly modified by where it is published. If reproduced on the cover of a museum catalogue — image equals art; placed on the cover of a "girlie magazine" — image equals pornography. It remains the same image, unchanged but substantially affected.

At this point, we must become concerned with another important influence on acceptance; to what degree is the image visually accessible? Perhaps the greatest factor affecting accessibility of an image is the balance between the viewer's perception and the image's depth of meaning. By exploring this symbiotic relationship we might better understand the effectiveness and acceptance of more successful images.

The concept that the artist has tried to convey to the viewer has been distilled into the final image. The image provides the viewer with subject matter and recognizable shapes or objects; these can be taken literally or as symbols. Although it is vital that the artist is effective in communicating the image's meaning, the accomplishment of understanding is equally dependent on the viewer's ability to perceive. Perception encourages an understanding of the meaning and relationships presented by the image.

One can think of a viewer's perception as being multi- dimensional and the image as having many levels of meaning. If the viewer interacts with the image in a single dimensional thought process, he/she might respond to various objects in the picture. This recognition is directly related to our level of experience and our ability to understand the fundamental meaning of the work. Responses such as, " Oh look, it's a nude woman" or " That's a lovely landscape" are evidence of a primary level of comprehension. This, by nature, is a sort of *seeing* instead of perceiving.

An example of exploring an image on multiple levels can be illustrated by looking once again at Judy Dater's ***Imogen and Twinka at Yosemite.*** The primary level is with subject identification. For some people, Imogen Cunningham and Twinka are recognizable and famous people. We are also presented with an attractive nude female figure, certainly of interest to a large segment of the population. There is an aspect of cleverness and humor to the image that is appealing and easy to comprehend.

As the viewer continues to respond to the image, the thought process may begin to attain a deeper level of investigation. Referring back to this work one can see the relationships of age/youth, mother/daughter or the classic art theme of artist and model. The image emanates an aura of fantasy. A nymph in the woods, discovered by an old woman, is reminiscent of a Brothers Grimm fairy-tale. For those well read in mythology, there are also references to Persephone and Pluto which the artist comments on in her statement. So we can see that the extent to which we investigate a photograph rests partially on the complexity of the image and in part on our willingness to explore it.

Let's say we have found a hypothetical image which fulfills the previously discussed criteria; it is appealing, understandable, accessible on many levels, and stimulates us intellectually and emotionally. We can assume this image will receive a general level of acceptance upon exposure to the public. But the formula is not yet complete. Another significant component is that of relevancy. Is the image timely and/or timeless? Does it provide us with a novel or better understanding of our psyche, our world or humanity? And if it does enlighten, educate, challenge or entertain us, will it continue to do so in the decades to follow?

Perhaps this is one area that decisively separates the artist from the mere image maker. Art is not only a process of discovery; it is also a procedure of refinement and clarification. As the human race evolves, its language, customs and society transform, dictating the re-evaluation of previously accepted symbols and terminology. The artist generates a new proposal, a blend of past and present. Whether this proposal receives long term acceptance is dependent upon it's significance of meaning and it's placement in humankind's visual history.

This requires the presence and effective use of certain elements. These are, on a more academic level, the resolution of formal concerns, original use of symbols, attention to aesthetic issues, and adeptness of technical ability.

In Ralph Gibson's photograph, ***Priest,*** we are able to see the formal elements presented in a resolved manner. The lines define simple shapes that are at once accessible to the viewer. The large dark mass at the bottom of the image is subtly divided by the black on black tonal variance of the jacket lapel and habit shirt. A noticeable texture change between the smooth black suit and the rough skin of the chin area is further accentuated by the unmarked surface of pale grey sky.

The religious significance of dark and light is evident, as well as the sense of rigidity discerned through the figure's squared shoulders and the almost stone-like texture of the firmly set chin. The tight relationship between the sky and jacket tones reiterates this theme metaphorically. A selective division of space provides an assymetrical balance giving the composition interest and a sense of tension. Aesthetically the photograph is harmonious and complex. All the elements are essential and are in correct proportion. We feel it to be "right" and therefore we are intrigued by it. But, from what source does this "feeling" originate?

In part, it comes from the psychological impact spatial relationships have on us. The contrasts in ***Priest*** are arranged with a sensitivity toward rhythm and tone, so that the end result is a unified amalgam of all the formal elements previously discussed. When we look at this photograph for its technical proficiency we can immediately see that the understanding of the medium is well developed in the artist. The evidence lies not only in his crisp visual imagery but also through his ability to print such a rich variety of blacks, whites, and greys. This expressive tonal range makes it as Ralph said in his statement, "almost a color photograph."

Ostensibly, creative people possess a higher degree of receptivity to imagery, symbols and metaphor. Their thinking appears to be flexible and adaptive. They combine ingredients from divergent origins and create innovative combinations of artistic unions. Often the artist discovers visual harmonies that we never knew existed, but are able to accept once they are revealed to us.

All of this is interesting, you might say, but what initiates the artist's creativity in the first place? Motivation can come out of a highly charged imagination, an unconscious need, personal experiences, or the desire to make contact with a deeper sense of self.

One of the creative sources mentioned throughout art history is the Muse. This muse or art spirit is recognized by many artists as an essential part of the creative process. Numerous writers, artists and philosophers have attempted to clarify this conceptual process which appears to increase the artist's awareness of the relationships between feelings from experiences, and visual symbols that might represent these feelings. The artist then uses these symbols to communicate his/her idea to the viewer. In essence, the artist has changed a concept into a *real* object. Many successful images are able to transcend time, ethnic and political barriers, age and socio-economic categories. It should be noted however, that as an artist refines his/her use of imagery, there is an evolution of style. "The artist establishes an area of exploration, not a series of unrelated creations." [10]

One of the reasons why photography is so popular and easily accepted is because it *mimics* reality. The various aspects of reality became complicated when we began to investigate the relationship between photography and reality. We considered this question with our artists and discovered some interesting viewpoints. When we discussed documentary photography with Mary Ellen Mark she commented, "Certainly the photographs that I do are reality . . . yet there is some sort of an abstraction and fantasy because of how I'm seeing it."[11] Duane Michals reminds us that reality is not limited to our physical world. He states, "the most important parts of reality are totally invisible . . . So I'm much more interested in what reality feels like rather than what it looks like."[12]

Throughout the history of the medium, artists have often done battle with the technology of the photographic process; a technology requiring that the object being photographed must at some point exist in the "reality" of the physical world. The camera is so well suited to capturing the "world out there," that it lends a greater believability to all it records. Many artists play with this aspect of the medium. Expressions of a uniquely personal reality may be more obvious to us when we see the work of Jerry Uelsmann or Val Telberg. These artists incorporate recognizable objects allowing the viewer to more readily accept the inconceivable in their constructed images. We know that ropes don't float above tables, but when we see a photograph of this imagery, we can accept the tangible reality of the familiar objects, even though presented in a fantastic situation.

So, we begin to see that photographers use physical reality only as creative material. Actually, they merge the corporeal with the perceptual to form a new reality. Artwork can exude a presence of its own and directly affect our consciousness with the same strength as tangible everyday objects. Regarding this concept of reality versus fantasy, Sigmund Freud stated, "An artist is originally a man who turns away from reality . . . He finds a way back to reality, however, from this world of phantasy by making use of special gifts to mould his phantasies into truths of a new kind, which are valued by men as precious reflections of reality."[13]

We must remember that the camera and photographer are selectively including, manipulating or eliminating objects. The lens mutates. It bends various rays of light at different rates. It can change depth perception, alter focus or change tonal qualities. It can compress or expand space and affect contrast. The photograph itself is real, but the photographic image is where reality and photography often part company. In photographs, the clouds will never rain, the people will never speak and the seasons will never change; but if accepted, the image will continue to exist, able to communicate its special message to us through the years.

So perhaps it was in our investigation of acceptance that we discovered some of the reasons for the popularity of an image. Acceptance basically means that we have embraced that which we understand, and this is for each of us a unique experience. The fact that the artist wants to communicate his/her feelings is well established by now, but it is our receptivity to it that is of equal importance. Which photograph will capture our attention and haunt us with its imagery and message? We never know for sure, but the excitement of discovery is always waiting with the next photograph we explore.

Steven Carothers and Gail Roberts
Boca Raton, Florida, 1989.

The following interview questions were selected to share some of the artists' personal views about photography and how it relates to their lives. By reading these excerpts, we hope that the unique views of the artists, and the sometimes surprising consistency of answers, will precipitate your own exploration of these questions.

WHAT IS THE BEST DEFINITION YOU COULD OFFER FOR PHOTOGRAPHY?

Bruce Barnbaum

- *Photography is a form of non-verbal communication. (First sentence of my book, The Art of Photography.)*

Judy Dater

- *I think it was Moholy-Nagy that said: "Photography uses light, a light modulator, and light sensitive materials." It still is the best definition that I know.*

Andreas Feininger

- *I see in photography the ideal medium of universal communication because it is independent of language and alphabet. Hence, a photograph can be understood anywhere in the world. To me, photography is the language of vision.*

Sandi Fellman

- *I think about the medium of photography as quite literally "drawing with light," the possibilities of which range from documentation to the farthest reaches of one's imagination.*

Robert Fichter

- *Anything that responds to light. I don't limit photography to the lens formed image as most people do.*

Ralph Gibson

- *We still have no acceptable definition for photography. I've said many times that it's like electricity; we know how to use it, but we don't really know what it is.*

Les Krims

- *Photography is a process with which one can most easily produce the best two dimensional illusion of reality possible.*

Sally Mann

- *Photography, like Wallace Stevens' jar, helps to reconcile life's airy intangibles and its durable matter.*

Mary Ellen Mark

- *That is an extremely difficult question — what kind of photography?*

Anyway, I think that a photograph is about an idea or point of view — somewhere in between painting or drawing and writing. Perhaps it is more like writing, I'm not sure.

Tom McCartney

- *Photography is not only the craft of making a photograph, but it also serves as a means of creativity and self-expression for the photographer. It's these characteristics that allow photography to establish its legitimacy in the art world. Photography is both the art and craft of creating a photographic image.*

Sheila Metzner

- *Time travel. Photography revolves around the theme of objects in time and space. A man, a metal sphere, a fruit, buildings, landscapes, plucked, ripe and perfect in its moment, captured and transported to the present perfect, the infinite, eternity, the future.*

Joel Meyerowitz

- *Light on the water, wind through the trees, dust on a butterfly's wings; all ephemeral but potent when observed. Photography describes what awareness observes.*

Duane Michals

- *I think essentially photography is a method of preserving and reproducing one's experience with relatively great accuracy — two-dimensionally.*

Bea Nettles

- *To me, it is anything that utilizes light sensitive materials. This would include traditional and yet to be invented chemical processes as well as electrostatics and digital imaging.*

Beaumont Newhall

- *A medium for the visual presentation of the world and its inhabitants.*

Arnold Newman

- *There is no "best" or definitive definition. If so we would know everything there is to know. We are forever seeking solutions to new ideas with our medium — as all art forms do.*

Olivia Parker

- *Photography is a visual language written in light.*

Eva Rubinstein

- *I doubt whether I could do better than a decent dictionary, unless it be to burble something like . . . lucid dreams caught in silver, scribbled notes from one's subconscious, to be deciphered over time.*

Val Telberg

- *Photography is one of many categories of mirrors: glass, shimmering water, mylar, concave, convex, enlarging, reducing, distorting, static, moving, etc.*

Joyce Tenneson

- *Photography is light writing and everyone is telling a different story. Photography means different things to various photographers, depending on what their training has been. I've always been amused by certain political groups within photography which have tried to narrowly define photography to suit their own vested interests and philosophy. Fortunately, things have really changed the past few years — there is more openness and respect for differing points of view now. The definition of photography has expanded and that is a very healthy development.*

George Tice

- *A way of making pictures that are more realistic than any other medium.*

Jerry Uelsmann

- *Photography is light remembering itself.*

Jack Welpott

- *Regarding my definition of photography I would prefer to fall back on Moholy for a definition. He said something to the effect that Photography consists of light, light sensitive materials, and the modulation of light. This definition leaves room for all the many plural ways photographs are made. There is a thing that I call Camera Work (shades of Alfred Stieglitz) which requires the use of a camera. I liken the camera to a musical instrument (oboe?); very easy to pick up, but very hard to play well. Some have said of the Oboe that it is an ill wind that no one blows well. In my view only a handful of people play the camera well, yet nearly every one has one.*

Cole Weston

- *A method for self-expression.*

WHAT RELATIONSHIP DO YOU FEEL EXISTS BETWEEN PHOTOGRAPHY AND REALITY?

Ruth Bernhard

- *Photography is reality. That is, we use all the parts of the world to make a photograph: a piece of paper that comes from a tree, that comes from a seed, that might have been brought by a bird. Then there's the silver in the image — that comes out of the earth. Then along comes the human mind that puts it all together. We must be careful about using the word "reality." The reality we humans know is only what we are able to perceive with our human senses. My sense of wonder at what is beyond is what I mean to express in my photographs. I have chosen to show discoveries, now transformed into photographic images, which in their total simplicity were a revelation to me. They are an attempt to express the infinite reality behind the commonplace, the miraculous inside the deceptively simple phenomena we see all around us with our limited senses.*

Judy Dater

- *Photography is both black and white magic, and it's the magic that still attracts me. Photography can create the "illusion" of reality, make people believe they are seeing some "real truth." In terms of representing the real world it editoralizes, selects, flattens, two-dimensionalizes, freezes, removes color, artificializes color, organizes, catagorizes, heightens or lessens, lacks taste, sound, touch, smell and temperature. It distorts.*

Andreas Feininger

- *Photography is the best mirror of reality we have. But similar to a warped mirror, or a mirror deliberately designed to distort, a photograph, too, can distort reality and, in unconscionable hands, be used for unscrupulous propaganda or other deceptive purposes. Therefore, one of the most important qualities of any good photographer is honesty in regard to his work.*

Sandi Fellman

- *There is a real scism between what we perceive and see, and what the "truth" may be if such a thing exists. Historically and culturally, we have come to accept photographic rendition as reality, validation and the truth. Those of us who are aware of the discrepancy between photographic representation and reality have both great power and great responsibility to work with the difference.*

Robert Fichter

- *Some images function as reality for people. I think all art that is successful is the same as reality. That is — it's transparent enough that the viewer who participates in it doesn't realize what it is, they just have an experience. They would not necessarily realize that they were looking at a photograph or painting, they'd just have the experience.*

Ralph Gibson

- *I don't want to make abstract photographs of reality; I want to photograph the abstract within reality!*

Les Krims

- *Photography is the ideal medium for making pictures if you are in love with the realistic illusion — literally.*

Sally Mann

- *A tenuous one.*

Mary Ellen Mark

- *I photograph reality — I have never been good at conceptualizing a picture or creating a fantasy world and then photographing it. But I think that I create my own point of view both by the way I choose to photograph my subjects and also by my choice of a frame in editing my contact sheets. I think all photographers create their own point of view or reality. So perhaps there is no reality in photography? I don't know.*

Tom McCartney

- *Anytime a three-dimensional subject is represented as a two-dimensional photograph, a departure from reality occurs. It is to what extent this deviation occurs that becomes the issue. Certainly a color photograph can be made to mimic reality with uncanny accuracy, but for me black and white photography is more challenging and exciting because a greater degree of abstraction takes place. Translating the reality of color into various shades of gray, coupled with the ability to change subject contrast, densities and tonal ranges, provides the means for greater creativity. Black and white photography now takes on a magical quality by giving a mystical sense of aesthetics to reality.*

Sheila Metzner

- *The photograph has its own reality. It lives as the subject lived in its own time. In its new space it has become its own form — that of a photographic reality. But it is real in that it came out of the illusion of reality. A painting can never achieve this ultimate power of photography which is to capture directly from life and to transform actual life.*

Joel Meyerowitz

- *A photograph is not separate from reality. It is made in the moment and is of the moment. Later while we hold and scan a print in our hands that moment inserts itself back into the flow of what we call the present. Image and description, like the printed word, evoke our response and stimulate our awareness. Whatever does that is part of our reality.*

Duane Michals

- *That's a central issue. Most people think that photography duplicates reality. Of course the question of what is real goes well beyond Plato. If one believes that the reproduction of observable facts is reality, which most people tend to believe, then I live on an entirely different planet than they do. My idea of reality is multi-dimensional. I don't believe in facts. That's the central problem I have, that the nature of something is quite different than the way it looks. For example, if you photograph a dead person — that tells you what death looks like, but it doesn't tell you anything important about the metaphysical nature of death or the implications of death in the most profound sense. So the most important parts of reality are totally invisible. They're what you feel. If I can photograph a women crying — that's like the tip of the iceberg — what's ultimately much more important and devistating is why she's crying. So I'm much more interested in what reality feels like rather than what it looks like. (DO YOU FEEL THAT'S POSSIBLE?) No, I fail constantly. If you want to reproduce a sunset, a moonrise, an automobile or a women's breast, if that's the nature of your inquiry, then that's not so hard to do. But if you want to talk about loss, or anxiety or nightmares or how it feels when somebody you love walks out on you, then photographs become approximations.*

Bea Nettles

- *Our belief that photography is real is what has always fascinated me about the medium. This trust is what makes one respond to it in ways not possible with drawing/painting. Most people familiar with the medium realize that photography is also interpretive . . . that a wide variety of choices affect its representative function. Any number of factors enter into this, from choice of lens, contrast of paper, cropping, point of view, sequencing, use of text, and the context the work is shown in. This is not even mentioning the fact that most photographs as we know them are two dimensional whereas the "reality" out there in front of the lens often has at least three dimensions and is constantly changing as it functions in time.*

Beaumont Newhall

- *This depends entirely upon the photographer.*

Arnold Newman

- *Only what we as individuals make of it. Actually photography is not real at all. It is only an "illusion of reality."*

Olivia Parker

- *What is real is supposed to be in front of my camera. I see it. The film in my camera sees it. The photograph is a transformation after reality.*

Eva Rubinstein

- *It depends on the photographer's relationship with reality. (And what, by the way, is reality?)*

Val Telberg

- *Photography has a quality of being able to serve as evidence of reality. In my work I stretch the word reality to cover thought, emotion, dream and even daydream.*

George Tice

- *One is the subject and one is the product. The fisherman has the sea and he pulls up fish from it. That's where I work, out there, and that's where I pull these pictures out of. So the work is very limited, just these brief moments. The reality is the constant thing of life.*

Jerry Uelsmann

- *A symbiotic relationship exists between photography and reality. Relative to my personal growth, I feel that the total camera experience provides a very special way of relating to and understanding the world. Above all else, the camera is a license to explore, a stimulus that tempts us to interact with the environment. The mere possession of a camera tends to heighten our perceptual awareness. With our cameras we can intensely and personally examine fragments of the world around us without feeling self-conscious. A crack in the sidewalk may provide a visual stimulus with poetic and enigmatic implications. Furthermore, one can interact without the need to articulate.*

Todd Walker

- *Only the relationship that may be in the eye of the beholder.*

Jack Welpott

- *Photography has the potential to mirror reality. That's what they thought it was originally. But it's a very inexact mirror, and we've begun to realize that the photographer's psychology, feelings, attitudes and so many things get into it. It's highly editorialized. I don't believe the idea that the picture is the truth. It is a truth generated by the feelings of the photographer. But also, it can be a total metaphor and operate like poetry. The object shown, the thing depicted, can only be a vehicle to some larger meaning. A little bit like the way a good poet can take the most common words, just little one syllable words, and put them together so they add up into something much beyond what those simple little words mean. I feel that way about photographs. The photographer can walk in and photograph common objects and transcend them, take them right beyond their literal meaning into some kind of poetic realm. I think if more people understood this, photography would be better served. They might look at it longer, instead of floating past in thirty seconds as they generally do.*

Cole Weston

- *With photography you can express the essence of reality.*

HAVE YOU EVER CONSCIOUSLY TRIED TO PROMOTE A PARTICULAR IMAGE IN ORDER TO INCREASE ITS RECOGNITION OVER THE OTHERS?

Bruce Barnbaum

- *No.*

Ruth Bernhard

- *I never have. I have always loved what I was doing so much that I didn't need to promote myself.*

Judy Dater

- *No, I am only interested in getting new work seen. When given the opportunity to pick an image for reproduction I like to pick something recent, that has personal appeal, and that I think will reproduce well. Most artists are interested in what they are working on at the moment, and once they decide the work is complete, want to get it out in the world somehow. Having it reproduced is a good way to do this and will reach a wider audience than those who come to see the work in a museum or gallery.*

Andreas Feininger

- *I don't quite know how to answer this question. As an artist, I feel free to use any graphic means to create the strongest impression of the subject of my picture. This has little to do with photo-technique because the technically most perfect photograph can be the world's most boring picture. I consider the ability to see creatively — to see in terms of photography — the most important quality of any photographer.*

Robert Fichter

- *I know that it's possible to do that. If you look at* ***Moonrise Hernandez,*** *you see the reason that it went up so astronomically in price is that everybody suddenly realized that it became a cultural icon. So if you had an image break through like that it'd be great, but on the other hand, I don't have time to deal with all that. Essentially, what you have to do is pick one style and stick with it so that your gallery can use that style as an icon itself. I don't like to do that.*

Ralph Gibson

- *I have others (photographs) that I am consciously reproducing in posters and postcards. The picture on the cover of Tropism, I have consciously reproduced that to get it known via the media.*

Les Krims

- *My attempts at promotion have been to sell groups of interesting pictures. To do this I've adopted strategies of capitalism. I have tried to capture market share by offering well-crafted, interesting pictures at reasonable prices in order to sustain the costs of my picture making, and acquire technology to allow the production of competitively priced images. My sale price for a picture is based on a reasonable mark-up over production costs, not on synthetically established rarity, or the volatile endorsements of critics. I always believed that as people became more sophisticated in their knowledge of photography they would buy my work because they liked what they saw, and because the pictures were a reasonable investment which would appreciate significantly in value over the long term (for instance, a print purchased at the Witkin Gallery, 15 years ago for $45.00, recently fetched $1430.00 including commission, at Christie's — a 3100% profit on a modest investment even beats Fidelity's Magellan Fund). The investment is still modest — under $200.00 for recent work. Critics still find my work as objectionably unintellectual (which really translates as non-Marxist), and politically incorrect as they did 15 years ago. My work is in this book not because I loaned the pictures to the Boca Raton Museum of Art, but because I required the museum to buy them at a reasonable price if they wanted to use them in the exhibition and book. Since the museum purchased the work, I can't imagine a better endorsement for the value of these pictures.*

Sally Mann

- *No. To the contrary, I find myself urging people to look more carefully at the subtler, less popular images.*

Mary Ellen Mark

- *No, I don't. The strong photographs promote themselves. There is nothing I can do to promote an image. If a photograph is good, people remember it and editors pick it to be published.*

Tom McCartney

- *No. There is a great amount of personal involvement in each of my photographs which results from printing each negative to meet my own expectations and satisfaction. Once this criteria is achieved and I am satisfied with its visual message, I'll then let the photograph stand on its merits and speak for itself.*

Sheila Metzner

- *Some of my images are idols to me, objects of adoration. I feel that what they contain can more completely transmit my efforts and ideals — my sense of homage to life. They are a greater gift; a more sincere exchange for what I have taken. It is those I regard more highly and wish to have seen.*

Joel Meyerowitz

- *No.*

Duane Michals

- *I tend to push those ideas that are in the forefront of my mind at the moment. I don't like to show old things over and over.*

Bea Nettles

- *Not at all. If anything, I have made an effort not to have the same image reproduced again and again.*

Beaumont Newhall

- *No.*

Arnold Newman

- *I "promote" nothing in particular. The question reflects the "hype" and commercialism cursing all the arts today. I simply allow all my images to "speak" for themselves.*

Olivia Parker

- *No. I work prolificly because I'm fascinated by what I'm doing. It wouldn't enter my head to bother to do that.*

Eva Rubinstein

- *Certainly not.*

Val Telberg

- *I promote human figure as my favorite metaphore of human psyche.*

Joyce Tenneson

- *Absolutely not. In the case of* ***Suzanne,*** *it has been so much in demand, it has taken on a life of its own. I can't keep track of how many times it has been reproduced in the past two years, but it is staggering.*

George Tice

- *I think you make a classic by it being published over and over and exhibited widely. Finally you wear people down and they accept it. Whenever I have a retrospective, of which I probably have a few each year somewhere, I'm always pulling out the photographs I don't like anymore. Certain ones remain. Those two Amish Boys have hung in there for a long, long time.*

Jerry Uelsmann

- *No.*

Todd Walker

- *Why would anyone be interested in doing that?*

Jack Welpott

- *No, not consciously. There are photographs which mark turning points in my thinking and I suppose I want those works to be seen. It seems that every couple of years a new awareness presents itself and I follow that muse.*

Cole Weston

- *No, I do it for myself, hoping that the viewer may, in some small measure respond to what I have seen.*

WHO DO YOU SEE AS YOUR MOST DEVOTED AUDIENCE?

Ruth Bernhard

- *Well, interesting enough, my photographs appeal to women a great deal, and it astonishes men because men don't quite understand what makes these photographs, my nudes, so exceptional. What did I do that they don't do? And the whole innocence and cleanliness of it, you know the unsexiness of it. It just surprises men very much, and men have said to me that they like the photographs so much because I honor women.*

Judy Dater

- *I think my audience has changed over the years, as my work has changed. I would like my audience to be people from a variety of backgrounds, with an interest and knowledge in all the visual arts, not just photography.*

Andreas Feininger

- *The people who are interested in the kinds of subject I photograph.*

Sandi Fellman

- *I believe I have a very diverse audience. People come to know my work through various channels; the art world, the photo world and academia, the world of editorial and advertising photography and recently through books (The Japanese Tattoo) and other anthologies. My devotion belongs to my artwork, but where my audience comes from, I couldn't say.*

Robert Fichter

- *A very small group of totally insane people who have happened upon my work.*

Ralph Gibson

- *At this period I must say that perhaps the French are most interested in my efforts — and by this I mean not just photographers but also elements of the general public.*

Les Krims

- *A few years ago I published an original print portfolio called "Idiosyncratic Pictures." The title of the portfolio not only described the kind of picture I felt I was making, but was also a direct taunt at ideologues who were promoting marxist strategies such as plagiarism in art, under the banner of Post Modern Appropriation. I believe my audience is composed of people very much like myself, who are idiosyncratic in nature, and share some of the views expressed in my pictures about life in this world. They are independent politically, and pragmatic philosophically. They love to be alive, are critical of hypocrisy, and enjoy good humor.*

Sally Mann

- *The captive one: my family.*

Mary Ellen Mark

- *I hate the word "devoted" and I would not like to limit my audience to any particular age, sex, or social economic group. I just hope that people will look at my photographs and be somehow moved or interested by what they see. Perhaps then they will be more open minded about things they have not seen or considered before.*

Tom McCartney

- *I have no idea. I can only assume it's the person who enjoys traditional black and white photography. I do know the highest level of devotion is when a person feels strongly enough about a particular image to include it in his or her collection. This is also one of the ultimate compliments a photographer can receive.*

Sheila Metzner

- *Anyone who loves life and quality craft photography.*

Joel Meyerowitz

- *Other photographers.*

Duane Michals

- *I have no idea — my mother? Mostly relatives. I know I have a constituency but I'm not sure exactly who they are.*

Bea Nettles

- *My work appeals to a very mixed audience which I find impossible to characterize. I do feel that the majority of people who know my work, know it through reproductions of it found either in books, articles or slides. These people by far outnumber those who have visited exhibitions.*

Beaumont Newhall

- *People who have an interest in the history and development of photography.*

Arnold Newman

- *Painters, photographers, sculptors and designers have always been my most devoted audience. They have greatly encouraged me from the very first and to this day have invited me to exhibit, lecture and teach all over the world. I must add my wife and my sons to this group. They have always kept my feet on the ground.*

Olivia Parker

- *I get the most consistent response from photographers and other artists.*

Eva Rubinstein

- *My mother.*

Val Telberg

- *I think persons who are both psychologically minded and involved in modern art, poetry and fiction writing. My main antagonists are straight photographers, non-objective painters and documentary writers.*

Joyce Tenneson

- *People who think for themselves, and are not threatened by opening and exploring their inner feelings seem most interested in my work. People are rarely neutral about my work — usually they are either moved by it or they feel threatened — there is little in between response.*

George Tice

- *The people who buy my books, collect my prints, study at my workshops and attend my lectures.*

Jerry Uelsmann

- *My friends and individuals open to visual questions.*

Todd Walker

- *The work finds an audience, if anyone chooses to look, I presume.*

Jack Welpott

- *I don't work with an audience in mind. I work for myself and hope that what touches me will touch others. Sometimes it does.*

Cole Weston

- *Ones who respond to my work. It may be students, teachers, housewives or whomever. I don't think one can single out a particular individual who responds to a particular type of photograph.*

POPULAR AND PREFERRED

THE IMAGES

Bruce Barnbaum

Basin Mountain, Approaching Storm, 1973

Gelatin silver print

38.8 x 49.4 cm (15.28 X 19.45 in.)

Popular

Bruce Barnbaum

Circular Chimney, Antelope Canyon, 1980

Gelatin silver print

49 x 38.9 cm (19.29 X 15.31 in.)

Preferred

Ruth Bernhard

In The Box, 1962

Gelatin silver print

19.6 x 34 cm (7.72 X 13.39 in.)

Popular

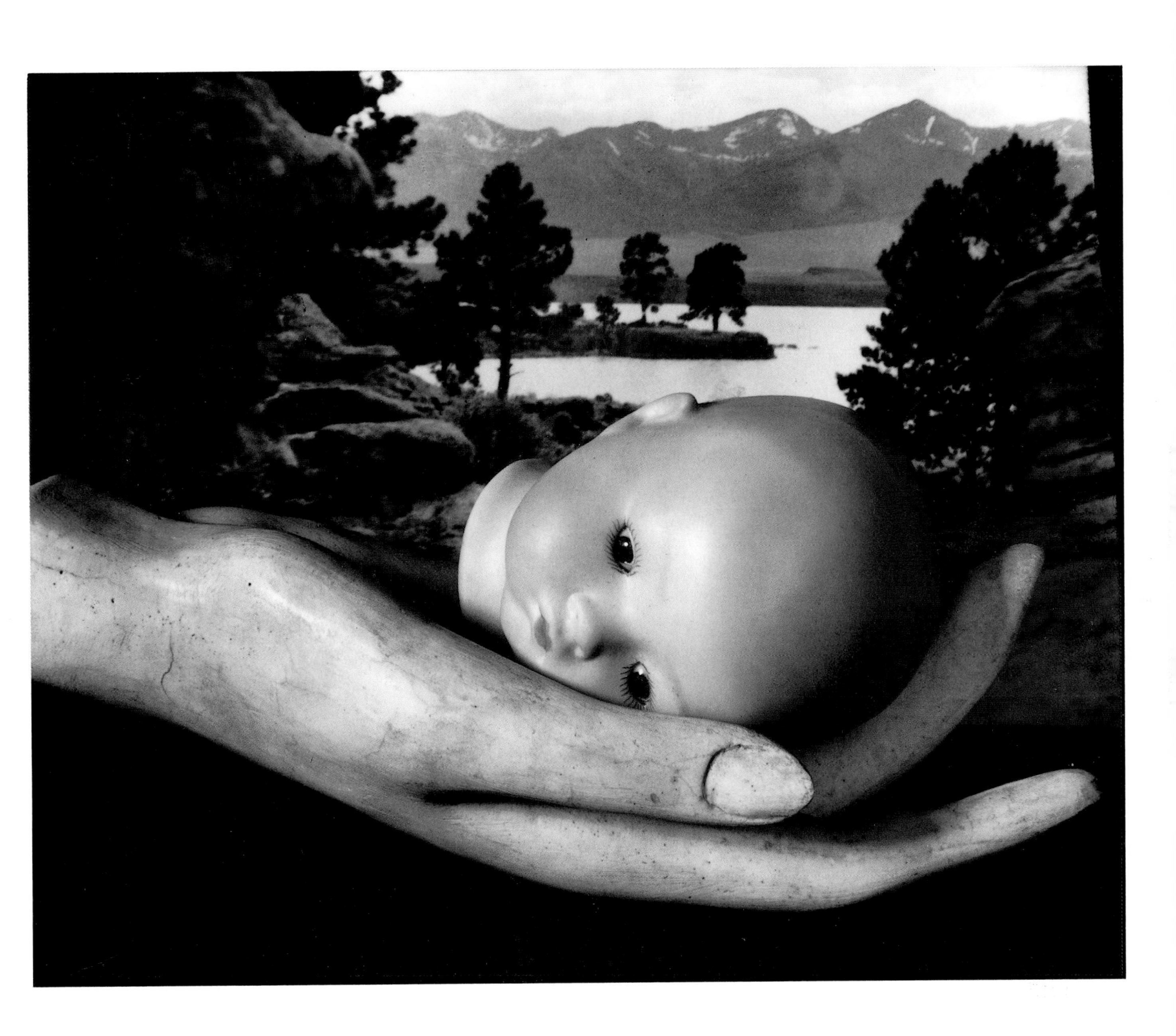

Ruth Bernhard

Creation (a.k.a.) Doll's Head, 1936

Gelatin silver print

19 x 23.5 cm (7.48 X 9.25 in.)

Preferred

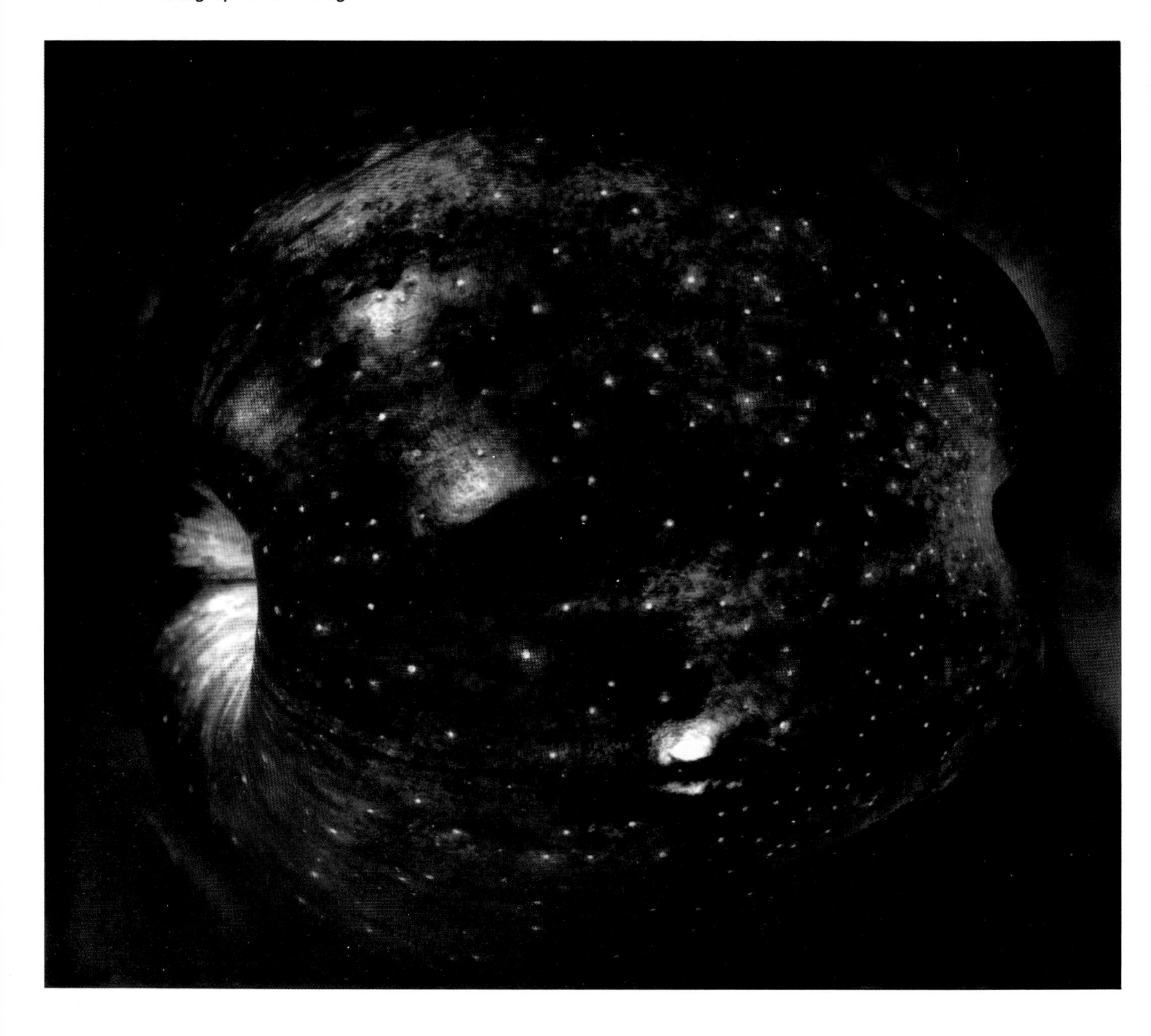

Paul Caponigro
New York City, 1964
Gelatin silver print
18.3 x 21.6 cm (7.2 X 8.5 in.)
Popular

Paul Caponigro

Rock Wall, Connecticut, 1958

Gelatin silver print

26.2 x 33.2 cm (10.31 x 13.07 in.)

Preferred

Judy Dater

Imogen & Twinka at Yosemite, 1974

Gelatin silver print

34 x 26.5 cm (13.39 X 10.43 in.)

Popular

Judy Dater

My Hands, Death Valley, 1980

Gelatin silver print

36 x 46.3 cm (14.17 X 18.23 in.)

Preferred

Elliott Erwitt

Moscow, 1959

Gelatin silver print

30.8 x 45.6 cm (12.13 X 17.95 in.)

Popular

Elliott Erwitt

California, 1955

Gelatin silver print

30.5 x 45.7 cm (12.0 X 18.0 in.)

Preferred

Andreas Feininger

The Photojournalist, 1951

Gelatin silver print

34.1 x 26.8 cm (13.43 x 10.55 in.)

Popular

Andreas Feininger

Broken Shell, 1971

Gelatin silver print

34.1 x 26.3 cm (13.43 x 10.35 in.)

Preferred

Sandi Fellman

Dragon Lady, 1982

Color photograph

60.96 x 50.8 cm (24 x 20 in.)

Popular

Sandi Fellman

Untitled, 1988

Color photograph

60.96 x 50.8 cm (24 x 20 in.)

Preferred

Robert Fichter

Standard Still-Life With Japanese Prints, 1982

Color photograph

89 x 73.2 cm (35 x 28.8 in.)

Popular

Robert Fichter

Turkey Puzzle

Color photograph

69 x 85 cm (27.2 x 33.46 in.)

Preferred

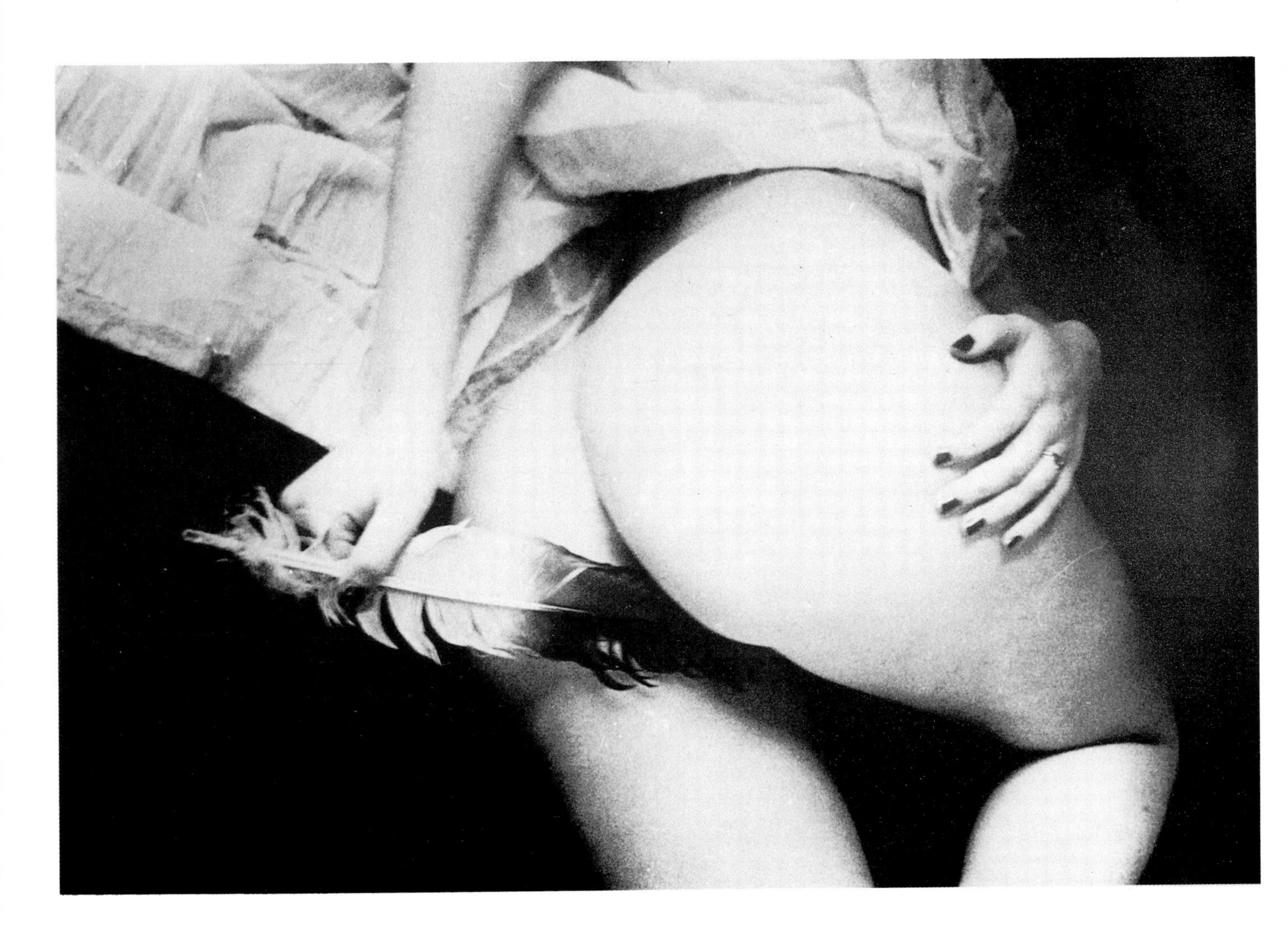

Ralph Gibson

Leda, 1974

Gelatin silver print

16 x 23.9 cm (6.3 x 9.41 in.)

Popular

Ralph Gibson

Priest (From Quadrants), 1975

Gelatin silver print

20.6 x 31.4 cm (8.11 x 12.36 in.)

Preferred

Les Krims

Mary's Middle Class, 1985

Color photograph

45.2 x 56.8 cm (17.8 x 22.36 in.)

Popular

Les Krims

Carla Lavorchik, 1988

Color photograph

45.2 x 56.8 cm (17.8 x 22.36 in.)

Preferred

Sally Mann

Untitled, 1979

Platinum print

24.2 x 18.4 cm (9.53 x 7.24 in.)

Popular

Sally Mann

Jessie At Six, 1988

Gelatin silver print

50 x 59.8 cm (19.69 x 23.54 in.)

Preferred

Mary Ellen Mark

Tiny, In Seattle, 1983

Gelatin silver print

33.7 x 22.4 cm (13.27 x 8.82 in.)

Popular

Mary Ellen Mark

Damm Family In Car, Los Angeles, 1987

Gelatin silver print

26.2 x 26 cm (10.31 x 10.24 in.)

Preferred

Tom McCartney

Mount McKinley, Alaska, 1982

Gelatin silver print

38 x 48 cm (15 x 19 in.)

Popular

Tom McCartney

Eventide, Maine, 1983

Gelatin silver print

31.7 x 25.4 cm (12.48 x 10 in.)

Preferred

Sheila Metzner

Joko Passion, 1985

Fresson print

41.8 x 62.7 cm (16.46 x 24.69 in.)

Popular

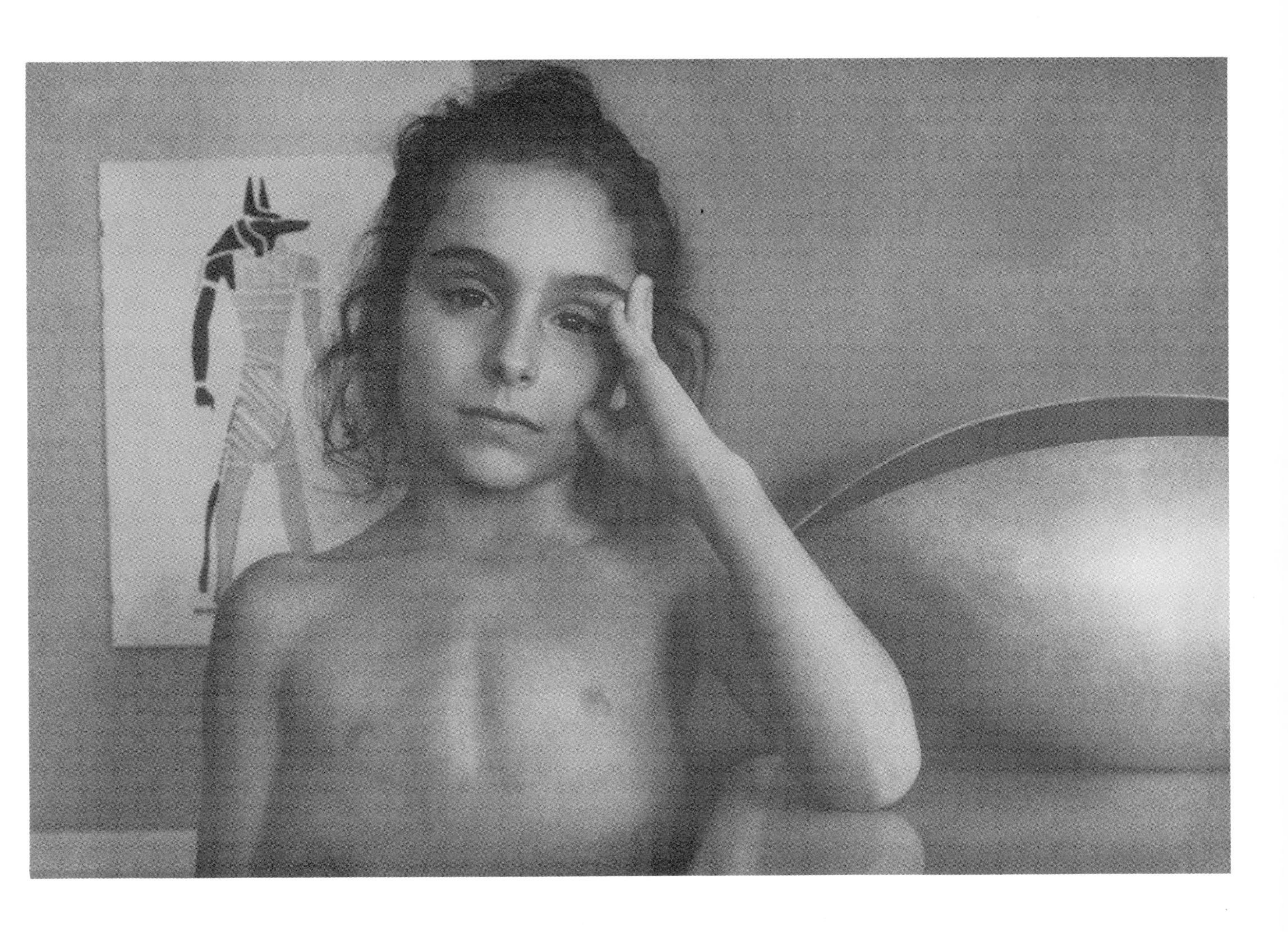

Sheila Metzner

Stella, Moulle Shapes, 1986

Fresson print

41.7 x 62.5 cm (16.42 x 24.61 in.)

Preferred

Joel Meyerowitz

Hardwig House, 1976

Color print

20.32 x 25.4 cm (8 x 10 in.)

Popular

Joel Meyerowitz

The Chateau, 1976

Die Transfer print

30.48 x 45.72 cm (12 x 18 in.)

Preferred

ALL THINGS MELLOW IN THE MIND
A SLEIGHT OF HAND, A TRICK OF TIME
AND EVEN OUR GREAT LOVE WILL FADE,
SOON WE'LL BE STRANGERS IN THE GRAVE

THAT'S WHY THIS MOMENT IS SO DEAR,
I KISS YOUR Lips AND WE ARE HERE
SO LET'S HOLD TIGHT AND TOUCH AND FEEL
FOR THIS QUICK INSTANT, WE ARE REAL.

Duane Michals

All Things Mellow In The Mind, 1987

Gelatin silver print

12.5 x 18.9 cm (4.92 x 7.44 in.)

Popular

Duane Michals

Illuminated Man, 1968

Gelatin silver print

17 x 25.3 cm (6.69 x 9.96 in.)

Preferred

Bea Nettles

Feminine/Masculine, (From Life's Lessons), 1987

Polaroid print

70 x 55.5 cm (27.56 x 21.85 in.)

Popular

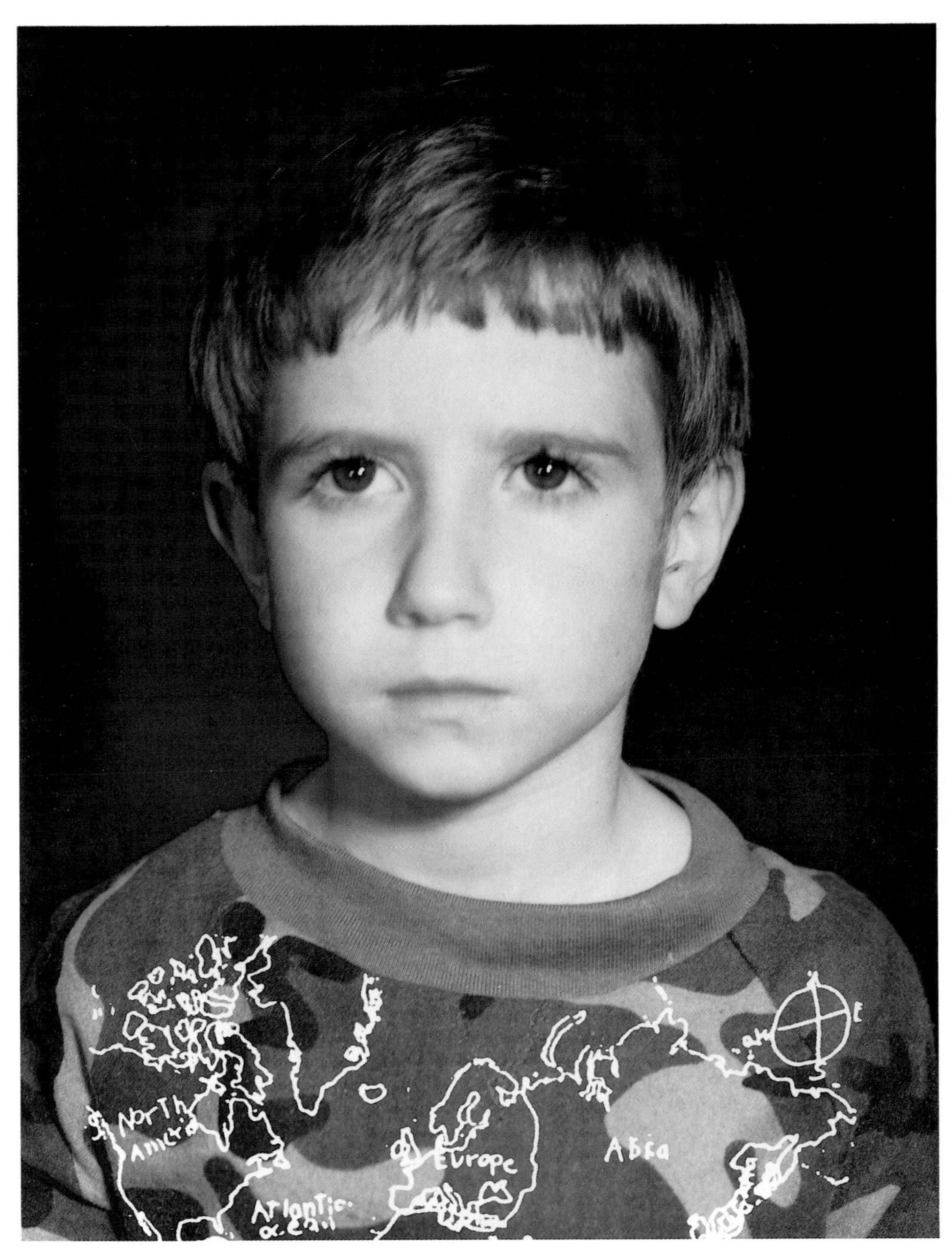

Bea Nettles

Gavin With The World, (From Life's Lessons), 1987

Polaroid print

70 x 55.5 cm (27.56 x 21.85 in.)

Preferred

Beaumont Newhall

Henri Cartier-Bresson, 1946

Gelatin silver print

30 x 42.1 cm (11.81 x 16.57 in.)

Popular

Beaumont Newhall

Mantlepiece, Schloss Leopoldskron, Salzburg, Austria, 1959

Gelatin silver print

26.7 x 26.2 cm (10.51 x 10.31 in.)

Preferred

Arnold Newman

Picasso, 1954

Gelatin silver print

31.8 x 25.1 cm (12.52 x 9.88 in.)

Popular

Arnold Newman

Sir John Gielgud and Sir Ralph Richardson, London, England, 1978

Gelatin silver print

28.9 x 31.4 cm (11.38 x 12.36 in.)

Preferred

Bill Owens

Reagan On T.V., 1970

Gelatin silver print

27 x 34 cm (10.63 x 13.39 in.)

Popular

Bill Owens

Companions Of The Forest Of America, 1974

Gelatin silver print

22.7 x 30.4 cm (8.94 x 11.97 in.)

Preferred

Olivia Parker

Pomegranates, 1979

Die Transfer print

18.6 x 24 cm (7.32 x 9.45 in.)

Popular

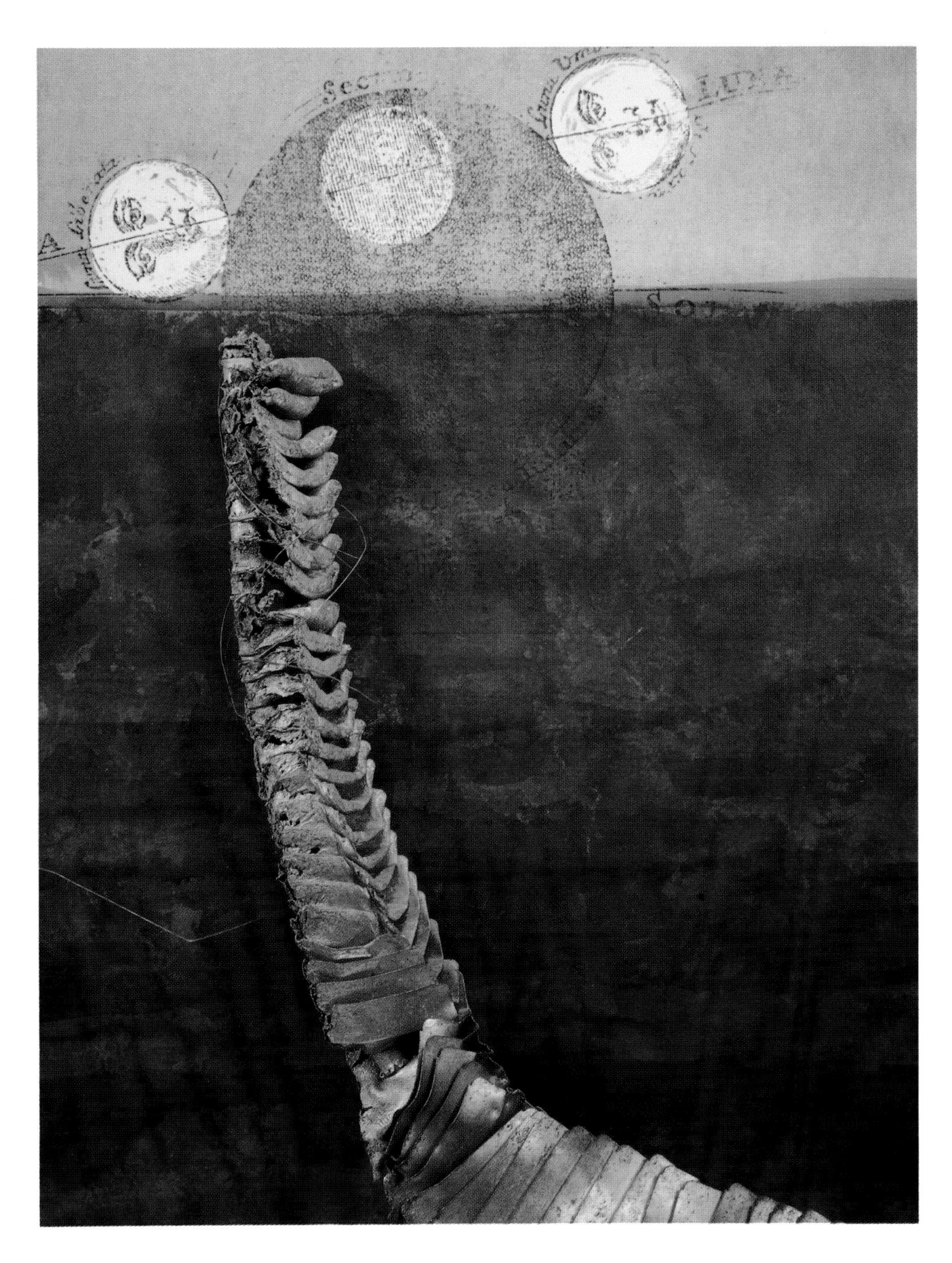

Olivia Parker

Moon Under, Earth Under, 1987

Cibachrome print

34.3 x 26.6 cm (13.5 x 10.47 in.)

Preferred

Eva Rubinstein

Bed In Mirror, Rhode Island, 1972

Gelatin silver print

19.7 x 29.1 cm (7.76 x 11.46 in.)

Popular

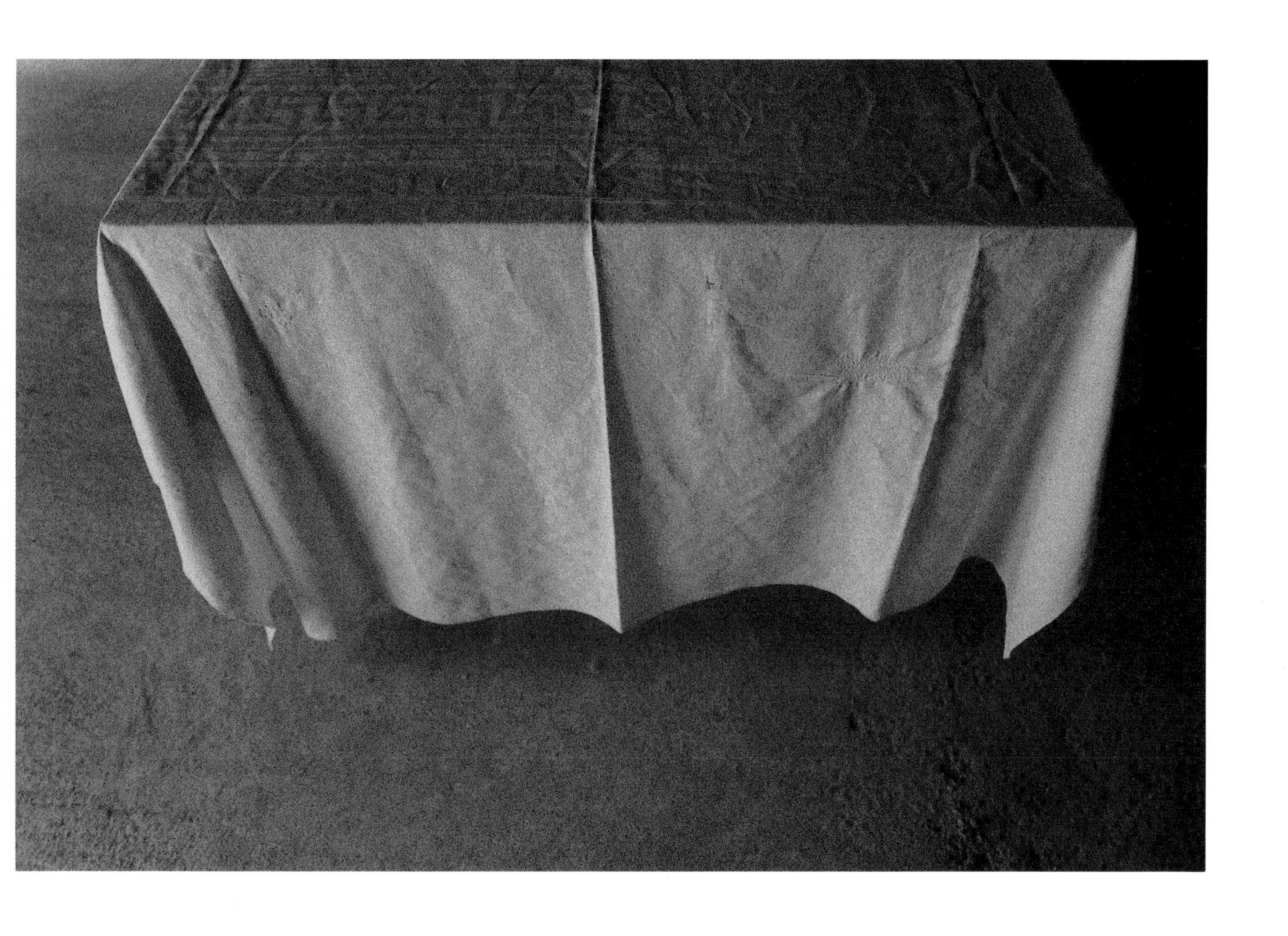

Eva Rubinstein

Table With Clothe, Arles, 1986

Gelatin silver print

20.5 x 30.3 cm (8.07 x 11.93 in.)

Preferred

Val Telberg

Men Listening, 1962

Gelatin silver print

27.2 x 35.3 cm (10.71 x 13.9 in.)

Popular

Val Telberg

Invasion, c. 1954

Gelatin silver print

24.8 x 19 cm (9.76 x 7.48 in.)

Preferred

Joyce Tenneson

Suzanne, 1986

Cibachrome print

60 x 50 cm (23.62 x 19.69 in.)

Popular

Joyce Tenneson

3 Women, 2 Men, 1 Child, 1987

Cibachrome print

59.5 x 50 cm (23.43 x 19.69 in.)

Preferred

George Tice
Two Amish Boys, Lancaster, PA, 1962
Gelatin silver print
28.8 x 19.1 cm (11.34 x 7.52 in.)
Popular

George Tice

Charlie and Violet On Their Houseboat, Jersey City, NJ, 1979

Gelatin silver print

26.6 x 33.7 cm (10.47 x 13.27 in.)

Preferred

Jerry Uelsmann

Untitled, 1976

Gelatin silver print

49.8 x 36.6 cm (19.61 x 14.41 in.)

Popular

Jerry Uelsmann

Untitled, 1981

Gelatin silver print

39.1 x 49.4 cm. (15.39 x 19.45 in.)

Preferred

Todd Walker

Torn Pair, 1981

Lithograph number 169

22.7 x 29.2 cm (8.94 x 11.5 in.)

Popular

Todd Walker

Untitled, 1969

Sabattier effect silver print

24.8 x 18.4 cm (9.76 x 7.24 in.)

Preferred

Jack Welpott

Sabine, 1973

Gelatin silver print

40.3 x 30.5 cm (15.87 x 12.01 in.)

Popular

Jack Welpott

65 Ave D'La Bourdonnais Paris, 1985

Gelatin silver print

33.1 x 42.6 cm (13.03 x 16.77 in.)

Preferred

Cole Weston

Surf and Headlands, 1958

Color print

40.3 x 50.9 cm (15.87 x 20.04 in.)

Popular

Cole Weston

Punts Les Quesnoy, France, 1983

Color print

39 x 49.2 cm (15.35 x 19.37 in.)

Preferred

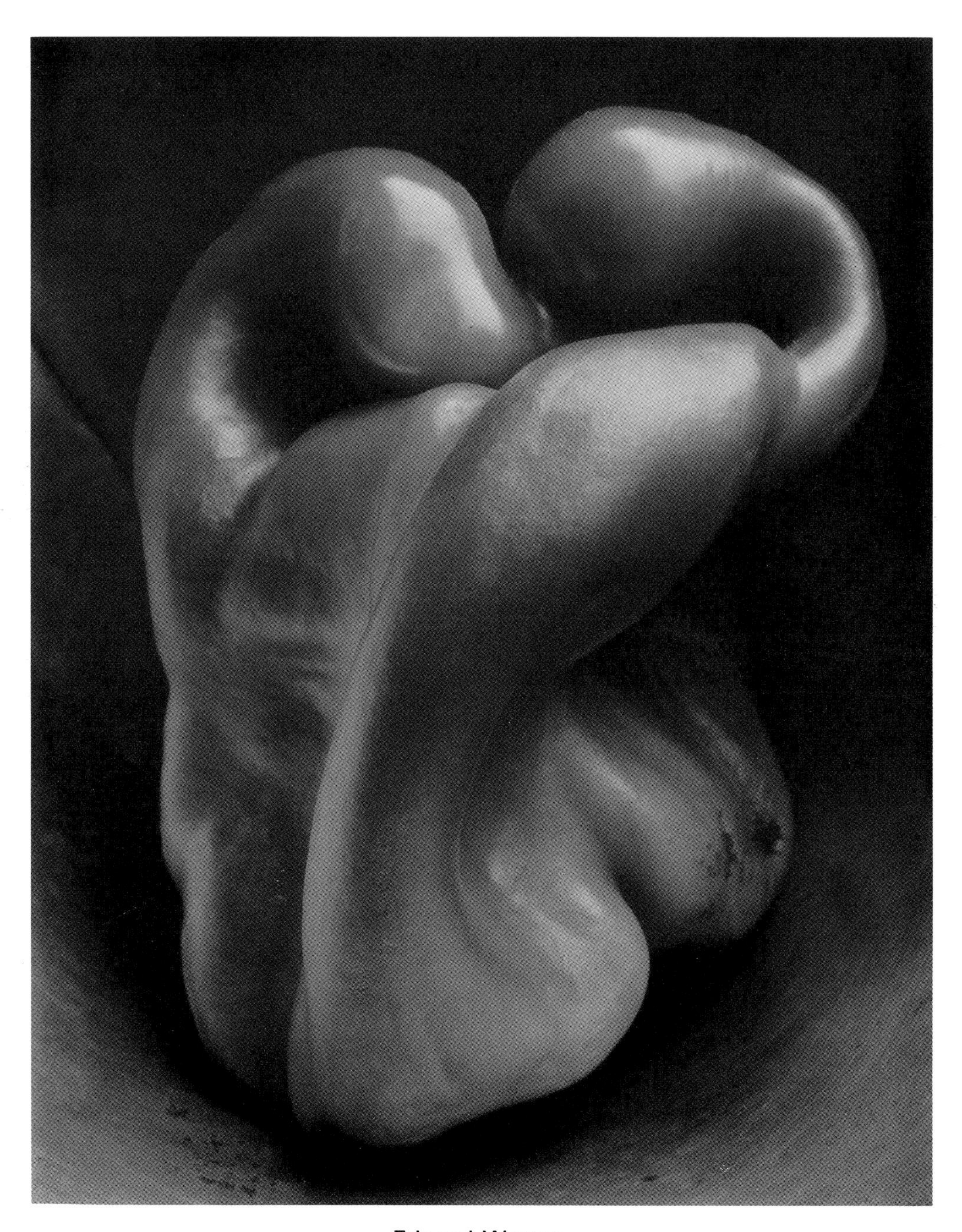

Edward Weston

Pepper No. 30, 1930

Gelatin silver print

23.7 x 18.8 cm (9.33 x 7.4 in.)

Popular

Edward Weston

Nude, 1936

Gelatin silver print

23.6 x 19.1 cm (9.29 x 7.52 in.)

Preferred

BRUCE BARNBAUM
Sonomis, California

Let me begin by saying that I am fortunate in having a favorite photograph that is also one of my most popular, and a most popular image that is also one of my favorites.

My most popular image is ***Basin Mountain, Approaching Storm,*** made on November 10, 1973. I was in the town of Bishop, California, to teach a weekend workshop for the Sierra Club when I stepped out of my motel for breakfast prior to the start of the workshop. Seeing the gathering storm clouds over the Sierra Nevada Mountains to the west, I immediately thought, "the hell with breakfast, this is more important!" I grabbed my camera, threw it in the back of my car, and drove north of town in search of a location that would provide a foreground worthy of the excitement in the distance. I found the spot about a half mile away. It seemed to all come together perfectly with the old western fence in front of the scene.

Over the years nearly 250 prints of this image have sold, making it my most popular photograph. To me it is very special because I respond so strongly to nature and to the interaction of its forces. I was hit by a surge of adrenaline when I stepped outside that morning, and I can remember that day so very vividly because of that heightened awareness and excitement. Later that afternoon, the storm hit hard, and we were forced to move the workshop to the town of Lone Pine, sixty miles to the south, the next day. There, I made another of my most memorable images, *Sierra Wave Cloud.* It was a very exciting weekend in every respect.

My favorite image is ***Circular Chimney, Antelope Canyon,*** made on January 2, 1980. It was the last day of a week-long trip with my wife, my dog, and several friends that took us into portions of southern Utah and northern Arizona. As we traveled from loca-
— continued on page: 134

BORN: Chicago, Illinois, 1943.

EDUCATION:
B.A., Mathematics, U.C.L.A. —1965.
M.A., Mathematics, U.C.L.A. —1967.

SELECTED ACCOMPLISHMENTS:
June 1975: Founded the Owens Valley Photography Workshops.
Nov. 1979: Published AFTERMATH Portfolio through the Stephen White Gallery of Los Angeles.
Sept.1981: Published Cathedrals of Man, a booklet of 24 images.

PUBLICATIONS:
Books:
Visual Symphony.
The Art of Photography, An Approach To Personal Expression.
Magazines:
Peterson Photographic, 1983.
Darkroom and Creative Camera Techniques, 1989.

RUTH BERNHARD
San Francisco, California

BORN: Berlin, Germany, 1905.

EDUCATION:
Ruth Bernhard studied art history and typography at the Academy of Fine Arts in Berlin.

PUBLICATIONS:
Books:
Ruth Bernhard: The Eternal Body.
Recollections: Ten Women of Photography.
Collecting Light.

I was photographing a friend and, briefly glancing out the window, saw a United Parcel Service driver carrying a very large box over his shoulder. I immediately envisioned her in it.

Since I knew the recipient of the package — which incidentally turned out to be her new 4x5 Omega enlarger — I had no problem acquiring the huge cardboard box.

I obediently followed my intuition and posed the model in the box, precisely as I had imagined!

It was not until ten years later that it suddenly occurred to me that this image might have come to me from reading D. H. Lawrence's book, The Man Who Died.

In The Box has become the Bernhard version of Ansel Adams' *Moonrise* — my most admired image.

Creation is the first image I made a year after meeting Edward Weston in California in 1935, and following my move from New York to the West Coast to study with him.

While browsing on Hollywood Boulevard, I spied this beautiful doll's head in the window of a doll hospital and decided I must have it. A few days later I discovered the plaster hand in a cigar store window, and I knew it was there for me.

Returning to my studio, I placed the head into the hand, then instinctively reached for the landscape of Silver Lake, Colorado, which I had only just printed, thus completing this symbolic image.

I strongly identify with this work, and through all these years it has remained my favorite.

PAUL CAPONIGRO
Santa Fe, New Mexico

I encountered the ***Rock Wall*** on route 44A while on one of my drives through the landscape looking for pictures. The road was being widened to accomodate the flow of traffic, and in the process a fresh cut was bulldozed from the low hill off to the side. The stone fractured in a way unique to this type of basalt formation. Attracted to the visual possibilities of what I saw, I pulled my car into a safe spot off the road and unloaded my camera gear to make some photographs. I exposed half a dozen negatives from various angles, but the one selected seemed to convey best what I felt about the place.

I had instituted a practice of hanging my finished or work prints on my wall so that I could see what had been achieved. Leaving the print on the wall for several days or weeks also allowed me the possibility of encountering the image at various times when my moods were subject to change. The print would look better or worse according to the reigning mood, but my object was to wait for those times when I was detached from the many moods and had reached a semblance of clarity and freedom for a more accurate assessment of the picture's worth. I found this method of approach invaluable to growth in my photography.

I hung this ***Rock Wall*** print near the entrance of my apartment for viewing. Time passed and one day as I was leaving to run some errands, I casually glanced at the image and was immediately struck with the importance of it. It was not important because I had made it or thought it to be a good photograph, but because it now appeared as a self-contained entity. In that unexpected moment the print spoke to me as if with a voice. The words were registered in my head or my heart, of course, but I was aware that my rational mind had not shaped that sequence of words which I now heard. It was as if
— continued on page: 134

SELECTED ACCOMPLISHMENTS:
1966: Awarded Guggenheim Fellowship to study ancient art forms in Ireland.
1978: Stonehenge, a portfolio, published. Received grant from Arts Council of Great Britian to photograph Northern England.
1982: Awarded National Endowment for the Arts grant.

PUBLICATIONS:
Books:
Paul Caponigro, an Aperture monograph, 1967.
Seasons, New York Graphics Society, Little, Brown & Company, 1988.
Megaliths, 1986. New York Graphics Society, Little, Brown & Company, 1986.
The Wise Silence: Photographs by Paul Caponigro, New York Graphics Society, Little, Brown and Company, 1985.

JUDY DATER
New York, New York

BORN: Hollywood, California, 1941.

EDUCATION:
1959-1962: University of California, Los Angeles.
1963: San Francisco State University, B.A.
1966: San Francisco State University, M.A.

SELECTED ACCOMPLISHMENTS:
1974: Dorothea Lange Award, Oakland Museum.
1976: NEA Photography Fellowship.
1978: Guggenheim Fellowship.
1987: Marine Arts Council. Individual Artist Fellowship.
1988: NEA Photography Fellowship.

PUBLICATIONS:
Books:
Judy Dater: 20 Years, University of Arizona, 1986.
Imogen Cunningham: A Portrait, by Judy Dater, New York Graphics Society, 1979.
Women And Other Visions, Photographs By Judy Dater And Jack Welpott, Morgan and Morgan, 1975.
Body And Soul: Ten American American Women, Judy Dater and Carolyn Coman, Hill and Co., 1988.
Magazines:
Artforum.
Camera Magazine.
Aperture.
American Photographer.

My most popular image, ***Imogen and Twinka at Yosemite,*** seems to have a life of its own. I made the photograph during a workshop where Imogen Cunningham and I were both teaching, and Twinka was modeling. It was time for me to do something, demonstrate the use of the view camera, speak to the students about using models, posing, directing. I had been watching Twinka walking nude through the woods with a bunch of students trailing after her. The idea to pose Imogen and Twinka together was inspired from a painting I had seen as a child by Thomas Hart Benton called *Persephone.* The subject of the painting is an old farmer peering around a tree at an unaware nude woman lying on a red cloth. It must allude to the myth of Proserpine (Persephone) and Pluto, God of the underworld, who sees her, loves her, and carries her off. The other part of the myth, which I was completely unaware of at the making of the photograph, is the loss and search for the daughter (Perserpine/Persephone) by the mother, Ceres, who is eventually restored to her. I see my photograph being not about voyerism, (the two women confront each other) but about youth and age, wisdom and innocence, mother and daughter. My original intent, however, was simple, to make a nice snapshot of these two people for myself, and as a class demonstration.

The photograph, ***My Hands, Death Valley,*** is one of my personal favorites because it marked a breakthrough or revelation about a new direction for me in my life and work. It was made not too long before turning 40, what I saw as my first mid-life crisis. I had been doing some traveling in the west with another photographer friend of mine, and while I waited for her to finish photographing, I sat in my car and stared out the window. I was noticing the way the landscape looked slightly different with and

— continued on page: 134.

ELLIOTT ERWITT
New York, New York

"Nobody was more anti-Nixon than I was, but I took a picture that some people think was very helpful to him. Westinghouse had sent me to photograph their refrigerators in 1959 at an industrial exhibition in Moscow. Naturally, in the Soviet Union, I was trying to see ten other photographic possibilities at the same time. Vice President Nixon was in town, rather stupidly saying things like "You eat cabbage and we eat red meat." Khrushchev got so annoyed he said, "Go screw my grandmother," an old peasant expression that sounds less offensive in Russian than in English but still means "Stuff it." (That was the true intellectual level of the famous so-called kitchen debate.) Nixon was playing for the U.S. press. Khrushchev was just being himself, because at that time the Soviets didn't have much press coverage of this informal type and didn't really understand public relations. My photograph delighted the Nixon crowd, of course, and possibly started William Safire's political career. He was doing PR for Macy's, but he saw instantly that this photograph could give Nixon the image he wanted, as the one guy "tough" enough to stand up to the Russians. Someone got hold of a print and it was used everywhere in the 1960 campaign . . . *without my permission.* I was angry, but I couldn't do anything about it. A few years ago, there was a reunion of the kitchen-debate alumni in Washington, and the *New York Times* photographed Nixon and me (I took the part of Khrushchev) recreating the scene. I don't hold grudges."

BORN: Paris, France, 1928.

SELECTED ACCOMPLISHMENTS:
Documentary Films:
Beauty Knows No Pain.
Red, White and Bluegrass.
Glassmakers of Herat, Afghanistan.

PUBLICATIONS:
Books:
Private Experience: Personal Insights Of A Professional.
Photographer, 1974.
Hundstage, 1988.
Personal Exposures, 1988.
Elliott Erwitt, 1988.

BORN: Paris, France, 1906.

EDUCATION:
1922-1925: Attended the Bauhaus in Weimar, Germany, served his apprenticeship as a cabinet maker.
1925-1928: Attended technical schools in Weimar and Zerbst, Germany, graduated summa cum laude as an architect and structural engineer.

SELECTED ACCOMPLISHMENTS:
1943-1962: Full-time photographer for Life. Designed and built several telephoto and close-up cameras which enabled him to achieve effects which were beyond the scope of commercially available equipment at that time.

PUBLICATIONS:
Books:
Nature in Miniature, Rizzoli, 1989.
Andreas Feininger, Photographer, Harry N. Abrams, 1986.
In A Grain Of Sand, Sierra Club Books, 1986.
New York In The Forties, Dover, 1978.
The Mountains Of The Mind, Viking, 1975.
Roots Of Art, Viking, 1975.
Shells, Viking, 1972.
Trees, Viking, 1968.
Forms Of Nature And Life, Viking, 1966.
New York, Viking, 1964.
The World Through My Eyes, Crown, 1963.
Maids, Madonnas, and Witches, Harry N. Abrams, 1961.
Total Photography, Amphoto, 1982.
The Complete Photographer, Prentice-Hall, 1965.
Total Picture Control, Crown, 1961.
The Creative Photographer, Prentice-Hall, 1955.

ANDREAS FEININGER
New York, New York

Broken Shell, 1977. Shells of this kind often have an inherent monumentality which, in my opinion, is comparable to the best in modern abstract sculpture. That most people don't see this is due to the fact that these specimens are rather small — only from one to three inches high. I deliberately photographed this shell in a way that made it impossible to guess its actual size. By this I hoped to destroy popular concepts about the insignificance of "broken shells", free the viewer's mind to see this common object of nature unbiased in a new light, and make him aware of its intrinsic beauty and power of expression.

SANDY FELLMAN
New York, New York

"In the summer of 1982, in my New York studio, I photographed my first tattoo. Immediately after Adrienne arrived, she peeled off her sundress and displayed an exquistely tattooed dragon down the length of her back. She told me, among other things, that for wedding presents she and her husband had given each other matching bat tattoos on their breasts. Adrienne also had rings in her nipples; she was exotic, and mysterious, and I was enthralled."

My fan piece is newest and is now one of a series of pictures shaped like oriental fans. This particular image however, I made almost two years ago. At the time I didn't know what to make of it and stuffed it in a drawer and forgot about it. Upon "rediscovering" it, its importance to me comprehendable, I knew how I wanted to present it and where to go with subsequent fan pieces. So it has a special significance to me and begins the "unfolding" of a whole new body of work.

BORN: Detroit, Michigan, 1952.

EDUCATION:
1976: M.F.A. in Art, University of Wisconsin, Madison.
1973: B.S. in Art, University of Wisconsin, Madison.
1972: Sir John Cass College of Fine Arts, London, England.

SELECTED ACCOMPLISHMENTS:
Polaroid Collection Grant.
1986 and 1987: Costume Design for Molissa Fenley and Dancers.
"The Photographic Vision" and "The World of Photography", Television broadcasts featuring Sandi Fellman.

PUBLICATIONS:
Books:
The Japanese Tattoo photographs and text by Sandi Fellman, Abbeville Press, 1986.
Legacy of Light, Alfred Knopf.
Blumen, Unschau Verlag Brieidenstein Gmbl.

Magazines:
Graphis: "Sandi Fellman, Beyond The Surface", by Amy Schiffman, Feb. 1988, Vol. 43.
American Photographer, "Exterior Decorations", Evelyn Roth, Vol. XVII, NO.II, Nov. 1986.
Camera Arts, "Against The Grain", Susan Brown, Vol. 2, # 9.

ROBERT FICHTER
Tallahassee, Florida

BORN: Fort Meyers, Florida, 1939.

EDUCATION:
B.F.A. University of Florida.
M.F.A. Indiana University.
Professor, Dept. of Art, Florida State University, 1983 to present.

SELECTED ACCOMPLISHMENTS:
Florida Fine Arts Fellowship, Jan. 1, 1981.
NEA Fellowship, 1979.
NEA Fellowship, Photography, 1984.

PUBLICATIONS:
Books:
Robert Fichter, Photography and Other Questions. Exhibition Catalog, published by Univ. of New Mexico Press and George Eastman House Museum.
After Eden, an artist book published by Univ. of South FL. Art Museum, Tampa, FL.

MAGAZINES:
A-X Cavation/RWF: A weapon to meet the terrible needs . . . text by James Huginin, illustrations by Robert Fichter, University of Colorado, Boulder, CO., 1988.

Standard Still Life was created in the back room of Harden's Taxidermy shop in Thomasville, FL. The most frequent question I am asked about this image is "Is the parrot alive?" Chuck Pittman, Pittman/Boris photography, Atlanta, GA., collaborated with me on this image. I wanted to use industrial standard lighting just like the folks who do the Coke ads. This is the mildest of the series of images created during a two day shoot. They have all been shown a number of times under the title *Apocalyptic Images.* The tougher ones really were prototypes for holograms to be installed at toxic waste sites.

Turkey Puzzle is part of an ongoing series of images that incorporate found imagery in the form of popular puzzle imagery with my own prints and photographs. The idea appeals to my need to recycle and layer the meaning of meaning. It was shot in my Tallahassee studio and deals with West meeting East and other culture shocks.

RALPH GIBSON
New York, New York

The earlier of the two is the woman with the feather. It is dated 1974, sometimes I entitle it ***Leda*** and the most interesting aspect of making the image is that it was made on the model's birthday. I was just shooting rather conventional nudes of her. By the bed was a vase of assorted feathers that Mary Frank had given me. A gamekeeper at the zoo gave Mary a large bunch of assorted feathers with which to paint in ink. She gave me a few and I made a bouquet etc. Anyway at a certain point the girl posing reached across and took one out of the vase and proceeded to caress herself. Being no fool I reloaded my Leica.

The ***Priest*** was made in 1975 and remains my favorite for several reasons. I was to make my New York debut in January 1976 at the Leo Castelli gallery. Although I had been showing around the world I wanted my show at Castelli to be something very special. I was preparing my series of images all taken at a three feet distance from the camera and entitled "Quadrants." I had carefully measured the gallery, a square room, and knew that it would contain 30 prints in 16"x20" size under glass only. No mat, no frame. All very concrete. I needed a full day to print one negative for the show and knew that I would have to stop shooting for the exhibit exactly 30 days before the delivery date of the prints to the gallery. On the very last day, a sunny Sunday morning, I went out with my Leica and met this priest coming back from celebrating the 12 o'clock mass. He agreed to pose and the image resulted.

The reason I like this image so much is that it positions me aesthetically exactly where I want to be. There is just enough reality, just enough formal quality, a frame as tight as a drum, etc. And although shot in B&W, it is almost a color photograph.

BORN: Los Angeles, California, 1939.

EDUCATION:
1956-1960: Studied photography in the U.S. Navy.
1960-1961: San Francisco Art Institute, California.
1961-1962: Assistant to Dorothea Lange.
1967-1968: Assistant to Robert Frank.

SELECTED ACCOMPLISHMENTS:
1988: Leica Medal of Excellence Award.
1987: Officier de L'Ordre de Arts et Lettres, France.
1985: John Simon Guggenheim Memorial Fellowship.
1975: National Endowment for the Arts Fellowship.
1973: National Endowment for the Arts Fellowship.

PUBLICATIONS:
Books:
In Situ, Navarin, France, 1988.
Tropism, Aperture, NYC, 1987.
Days At Sea, Lustrum Press, NYC, 1975.
Deja Vu, Lustrum Press, NYC, 1973.
The Somnambulist, Lustrum, NYC, 1970.

LES KRIMS
Buffalo, New York

BORN: Brooklyn, New York, 1942.

EDUCATION:
The Cooper Union, New York, NY, B.F.A. June 1964.
Pratt Institute, Brooklyn, NY, M.F.A. February, 1967.

SELECTED ACCOMPLISHMENTS:
George Eastman House (one man), Rochester, New York, 1969.
Les Krims / Duane Michals, Musee National d'Art Moderne.
Centre Georges Pompidou, Paris, France, 1976.
"Idiosyncratic Pictures" (one man), Galerie Fiolet, Amsterdam, Holland, 1980.
"Photography, A Facet of Modernism," San Francisco Museum of Modern Art, San Francisco, California, 1986.

PUBLICATIONS:
FICTCRYPTOKRIMSOGRAPHS, Humpy Press, Buffalo, NY, 1975.
The Incredible Case of the Stack O' Wheats Murders, Humpy Press, 1971.
Idiosyncratic Pictures, Buffalo, New York, 1980.
Making Chicken Soup, Humpy Press, Buffalo, New York.
The Little People of America, Humpy Press, Buffalo, NY, 1971.
The Deerslayers, Humpy Press, Buffalo, New York.
Eight Photographs: Leslie Krims, Doubleday.
Magazines:
ZOOM, No.91, Paris, France.

I loved Charlie Chan movies when I was a kid! In my favorite, stiffs keep turning up who have obviously been shot — but their bodies never have an exit wound or a trace of a bullet. The brilliant Chan discovers that the fiend's weapon is an air gun, and that bullets literally melt and disappear after entering the victim's body because they are molded of frozen blood. "Frozen Blood Bullets" is a good title and an odd metaphor for a photograph.

Art, science, commercial photography, special effects, real life, movies, cartoons, and the cleverly crafted locutions of humor, have always provided stimulation for my picture making. Teaching photography and making photographs, have helped me to become an avid advocate of the medium's craft and expressive abilities, and — through my pictures — occassionally a critic of its uses, institutions and clerisies.

SALLY MANN
Lexington, Virginia

These two pictures represent the opposite ends of this particular aesthetic spectrum. My work appears to have turned irrevokably from the decorative to a commitment best described as humanistic.

Jessie at 6, however, is evidence that the documentary impulse I am yielding to need not be without occasional lyricism and grace. The best I can hope for is such a marriage; between the seemingly disparate elements of the document and the interpretation, a collusion between foresight and chance.

BORN: Lexington, VA, 1951.

EDUCATION:
M.A. Hollins College, 1974-1975.
B.A. Hollins College, 1972-1974.
Bennington College, 1969-1971.

SELECTED ACCOMPLISHMENTS:
The Guggenheim Foundation, 1987.
National Endowment for the Arts Fellowship, 1982, 1988.
Ferguson Grant, Friends of Photography, 1974.

PUBLICATIONS:
Still Time, The Photographs of Sally Mann, catalogue, 1988.
At Twelve, Portraits of Young Women, Aperture, 1988.
Second Sight, The Photographs of Sally Mann, David Godine, publisher, Boston, 1982.

Magazines:
Arts Magazine, review, 1988.
The New York Times Book Review, 1988.
Photo Design Magazine, review, 1988.
People Magazine, review, 1988.
Popular Photography, Profile, 1988.
The Village Voice, review, 1987, 1988.
Aperture Magazine, 1987, 1988, 1989.
Harpers Magazine, 1987, 1988.
Art In America, review, 1986.
Mother Jones.

MARY ELLEN MARK
New York, New York

BORN: Philadelphia, PA.

EDUCATION:
1962: B.F.A. in Painting and Art History, University of Pennsylvania.
1964: M.A. in Photojournalism, Annenberg School of Communiations, University of Pennsylvania.

SELECTED ACCOMPLISHMENTS:
1965-66: Fulbright Scholarship to photograph in Turkey.
1977: New York State Council for the Arts—CAPS Grant.
1979-80: National Endowment for the Arts.

PUBLICATIONS:
Books:
America In Crisis, Magnum, 1969.
The Photojournalist: Two Women Explore the Modern World and the Emotions of Individuals, Mark and Leibovitz, Thomas Y. Crowell, 1974.
Falkland Road, Alfred A. Knopf, 1981.
Mother Teresa's Mission of Charity in Calcutta, The Friends of Photography Untitled Series, 1985.
Streetwise, Univ. of Penn. Press, published in 1988.
Homeless in America, Acropolis Books, 1988.

Tiny, In Seattle, *1983.* This photograph was taken during the making of the film "Streetwise." Tiny, a teenage prostitute is dressed in her Halloween costume. When I asked her what her costume was, she told me she was dressed as a French whore. I selected this image for two reasons. First of all because many people respond to it, therefore it's one of my most popular images. Also because it is a reminder of Tiny, and the incredible experience of "Streetwise."

Damm Family In Car, Los Angeles, *1987.* This photograph was taken after spending a week with a homeless family in Los Angeles. It was part of a story for Life Magazine. For the Damm family, their old car was their home. In documentary photography the ideal photograph is one that truly visualizes the photographer's emotional feeling towards his subject. Also ideally, a photograph should be a metaphor that goes beyond that particular image. This is one of my favorite photographs because I believe it successfully shows how I felt about the Damm family; their loneliness, their desperation. I also hope that this family can stand as a symbol about how it feels to be homeless in America.

TOM McCARTNEY
Lantana, Florida

Mount McKinley — Alaska, *1982.* The Indians of Alaska gave the name Denali—"The High One" to this mountain. This is the highest mountain in North America (20,320 feet) and it's because of this dramatic rise that the mountain is usually found shrouded in clouds. Both peaks are only visable approximately twenty days a year with the best chance of visability at sunrise and sunset.

On this late summer morning, I left my campsite along the Teklanika River hours before sunrise to travel the fifty miles to Wonder Lake with expectations of a clear sunrise to photograph the north slope. Daybreak found a tremendous snowstorm attacking the higher elevations with several rainstorms in the lower elevations and surrounding foothills. The size and number of storms indicated they would probably be present most of the day. I slowly worked my way eastward towards the Muldrow Glacier bed and at 4:00 pm. the storms finally moved off to the northwest. The remaining light was flat with the exception of the higher mountain elevations.

I decided to try and show this mountain in all its majesty. Darkening the shadowed glacier bed and contrasting it with the numerous glacial rivers and streams would produce the richness and luster the print deserved. Brilliance would be supplied by maintaining the values of the sunlit snows while increasing the separation of the mountain peaks from the sky. This was accomplished by underexposing the film by 2½ stops while increasing the development time of the negative by forty percent. A medium yellow filter was also used to lower the shadow values even further while helping to increase the separation of the sunlit snow from the sky.

Eventide — Maine, *1983.* Autumn arrived early that year bringing — continued on page: 135

BORN: Grove City, PA., 1938.

EDUCATION:
B.S., Ohio State University.
D.V.M., Ohio State University.
Studied Photography with Ansel Adams, Gene Arant, George Tice, Minor White.

PUBLICATIONS:
Books:
The Zone System: Testing Procedures For All Formats, Morgan and Morgan, Fall 1989.

SHEILA METZNER
New York, New York

BORN: New York, NY, 1939.

EDUCATION:
Pratt Institute, Brooklyn, New York.
Life, Travel, Books, Art.

SELECTED ACCOMPLISHMENTS:
Mirrors and Windows: American Photography Since 1960.
Counterparts, Weston NAEF, Metropolitan Museum of Art.
Nude: Photographs 1850-1980.
Life Library of Photography, Time/Life Books, Photography Book of the Year.

PUBLICATIONS:
Books:
Objects of Desire.

Magazines:
Conde Nast Publications, Vogue, Vaniety Fair, House and Garden.

JOEL MEYEROWITZ
New York, New York

BORN: New York, NY., 1938.

EDUCATION:
Graduated Ohio State University, Columbus, Ohio, 1959.

SELECTED ACCOMPLISHMENTS:
1970, 1978, received a Guggenheim Photographer's Fellowship.
Won an NEA grant in 1978.
CAPS Grant in 1975.

PUBLICATIONS:
Books:
The City: American Experience, 1971.
Cape Light, New York Graphics Society, 1978.
St. Louis and The Arch, New York Graphic Society, 1980.
Wild Flowers, New York Graphic Society, 1983.
A Summer's Day, Times Books, 1986.

DUANE MICHALS
New York, New York

BORN: McKeesport, PA., 1932.

EDUCATION:
1953: B.A., University of Denver.
Freelance photographer, 1958-present.

SELECTED ACCOMPLISHMENTS:
1975: CAPS Grant.
1976: National Endowment for the Arts Grant.
1978: Pennsylvania Council of the Arts.
1979: Carnegie Foundation Photography Fellow, Cooper Union.

PUBLICATIONS:
Books:
Sequences, 1970.
Real Dreams, 1977.
Duane Michals: Photographs with Written Text, 1981.
Sleep and Dreams, Duane Michals Photographs/ Sequences/Texts 1958-1984.
Duane Michals, The Nature of Desire, 1986.

Magazines:
Modern Photography, Popular Photography, The Photo Image, Camera 35, Esquire, Newsweek, Artforum, Art in America, Photo (France), Arts Magazine, American Photographer, Camera Arts, Darkroom Photography

All Things Mellow in the Mind is a traditional momento mori, which illustrates my awareness of being and not being. It is about youth, our illusions of permanence, and our unawareness of the moment of now, which is all there is or ever will be.

The Illuminated Man illustrates my idea of enlightenment, in the Eastern sense by which one becomes what we are and have always been, but have forgotten — a joyous energy and light transcendent. This photograph was taken in a traffic tunnel under Park Avenue, where I had noticed a single shaft of light. By placing the man where the light would shine on his face only, I then exposed the film so that his face was obliterated in pure light. His energy was seen. He was it.

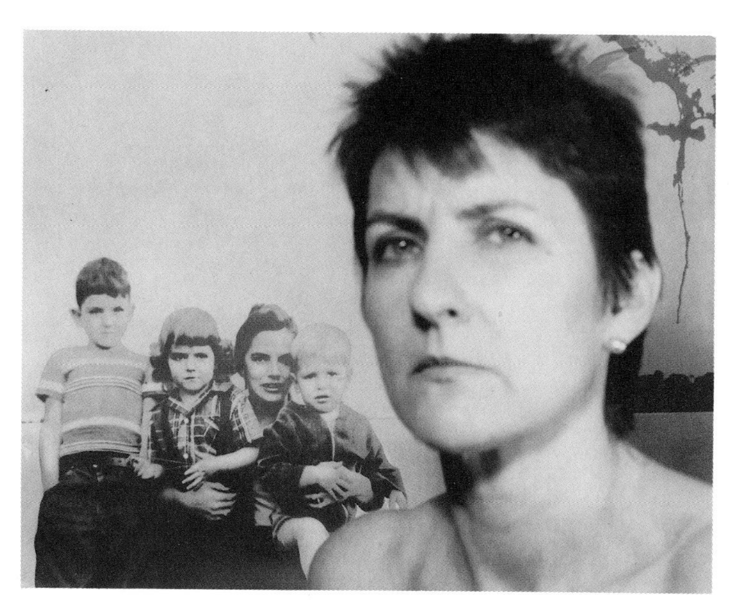

BEA NETTLES
Urbana, Illinois

These portraits of my two children were made on the same day. They became a part of a body of work entitled, Life's Lessons, a photographic treatment of important cultural and social themes. In this body of work I am revealing some of the difficulties and concerns of parenting, specifically the mother-child relationship. I deconstruct some of the stereotypes about mothering and hope to cause an examination of the process of raising children in this culture.

Life's Lessons touches upon universal problems of childhood such as fear of separation from parents, sibling rivalry, dealing with aggression, gender identification, the generation gap, and struggles with discipline and limits. I also deal with problems more intensely felt by today's children and their parents; materialistic values, fear of violence, and doubts about the future.

My personal favorite is the image of ***Gavin with the World.*** It was made in response to my negative feelings for camouflage clothes and GI Joe as role model. The map of the world was drawn by my son and fits neatly and somewhat heavily on my young child's chest. The weight of the world's problems bears down hard on the next generation.

More widely reproduced and therefore a bit more popular is ***Feminine/Masculine*** which features my daughter at age eight. Superimposed over her innocence is a list, in her own handwriting, of the feminine/masculine roles (a school exercise). The mistakes she made indicate that she is still absorbing these roles, and that some of them had no meaning whatsoever to her at that point in time.

BORN: Gainesville, FL, 1946.

EDUCATION:
1970: M.F.A. University of Illinois.
1968: B.F.A. University of Florida.

SELECTED ACCOMPLISHMENTS:
1986-89: Polaroid Corporation Artists Program.
1986: Ilinois Arts Council Fellowship.
1979 and 1988: National Endowment for the Arts Fellowship.
1976: CAPS Grant, NY State Council for the Arts.

PUBLICATIONS:
Books:
Breaking the Rules: A Photo Media Cookbook.
Flamingo in the Dark: Images by Bea Nettles.
Corners: Grace and Bea Nettles.

Magazines:
American Photographer, Popular Photography, Art News, Darkroom, Art In America, Afterimage, Arts Magazine Modern Photography.

BEAUMONT NEWHALL
Santa Fe, New Mexico

BORN: Lynn, MA, 1908.

EDUCATION:
Harvard, Cambridge, Mass., A.B., 1930. MA., 1931.

SELECTED ACCOMPLISHMENTS:
Curator of Photography, Museum of Modern Art, New York, 1940-45.
Curator, International Museum of Photography at George Eastman House, Rochester, NY, 1948-58. Director, 1958-1971.
Visiting Professor of Art, University of New Mexico, 1971-1984.
Fellow of the John Simon Guggenheim Foundation.
Fellow of The John D. and Catherine T. MacArthur Foundation, 1984-89.
Honorary Doctor of Arts, Harvard University, 1978.
Honorary Doctor of Fine Arts, State University of New York, 1986.

PUBLICATIONS:
Books:
On Photography, 1956.
Masters of Photography, 1958.
Airborne Camera, 1969.
Frederick H. Evans, 1973.
William Henry Jackson, 1974.
The Daguerreotype in America, third edition, 1976.
Photography: Essays and Images, 1980.
The History of Photography, 1982.
Photography and the Book, 1983.
In Plain Sight, 1983.
Latent Image, 1983.
Edward Weston Omnibus, 1984.
Supreme Instants: The Photography of Edward Weston, 1986.

Portrait of Henri Cartier-Bresson, 1946. Henri Cartier-Bresson came to New York in 1946 at the time of the exhibition of his photographs at the Museum of Modern Art. I was asked by Popular Photography magazine to write a profile of him. The editor then asked me to photograph him — my first and only journalistic assignment. I made this portrait of Henri in his New York apartment as we talked together. He had just acquired a new lens, of 85mm focal length and an aperture of f/1.5 — then very uncommon. He suggested that I try it out on my Leica. Over seventy prints of this portrait have been collected over the years since I took my friend's portrait, making it my most popular photograph by far.

Mantelpiece Detail, Schloss Leopoldskron, Salzburg, Austria, 1959. Schloss Leopoldskron, the beautiful Baroque palace built in Salzburg by the Archbishop Leopold Anton Graf Firmian between 1736 and 1744, is now the home of the Salzburg Seminar in American Studies. I was a member of the faculty in 1959 and was so impressed by the wealth of beauty surrounding me that I made many photographs interpreting the bold Baroque style and the masterful stucco-work of the building.

ARNOLD NEWMAN
New York, New York

Pablo Picasso. In 1954, I arranged with several publications for a series of assignments in Europe that would take six months. The European art world was also my destination. To my surprise, I found that European artists, for the first time, were looking to and being influenced by the American artists. I was plied with questions about them and their work. But the old masters were there in Europe and I began to photograph them. Leaving Paris I headed for Italy by way of Nice, hoping to see Picasso in Vallauris. I had forgotten our letters of introduction so I drew up a letter of my own, had it translated and waylaid him at the entrance of his home. At first he was visibly annoyed — he had become a tourist attraction. But the letter, purposely mentioning the names of many mutual friends, convinced him, and he asked me to return early the next day. He surprised me by recognizing my photographs and took me to his studio, cautioning me that he had a one o'clock appointment. When that hour arrived, I mentioned it. (His son, Paul, was translating.) He answered, "Stop talking so much and keep taking photographs!" About three o'clock, to our mutual disappointment, I ran out of film.

Sir John Gielgud and Sir Ralph Richardson. This is a photograph I had been planning to do for several years, ever since I saw them working together in Pinter's, No Man's Land. Their acting relationship, going back a lifetime, created a marvelous interplay that would have been a delight for any photographer to interpret. This picture was taken in an alleyway at the side of the Duke of York's Theatre, London, where Gielgud was appearing. I feel that it could almost be directed by Pinter. We were set up and ready when they came along rather happily after a convivial lunch. They sailed right into the spirit of the occasion and not only acted for me, but rather overacted. The most startling bit of business was Sir Ralph's imitation of John Wayne.

BORN: New York, NY, 1918.

EDUCATION:
1936-1938: University of Miami, Coral Gables, FL.

SELECTED ACCOMPLISHMENTS:
1951: Photokina Award, Cologne, Germany.
1961: The Newhouse Citation, University of Syracuse.
1975: American Society of Magazine Photographer's Life Achievement in Photography Award.
1981: Honorary Degree, Doctor of Fine Arts, University of Miami Coral Gables, FL.
1985: Missouri Honor Medal for Distinguished Service to Journalism, University of Missouri.
1989: Honorary Degree of Doctor of the University, University of Bradford, England.

PUBLICATIONS:
Books:
Bravo Stravinsky, 1967.
One Mind's Eye: The Portraits And Other Photographs Of Arnold Newman, 1974.
Faces USA, 1978.
The Great British, 1979.
Artists: Portraits From Four Decades, 1980.
Arnold Newman in Florida, 1987.

Magazines:
Life, Look, Esquire, Holiday, Harper's Bazaar, Travel and Leisure, Town and Country, Vanity Fair.

BILL OWENS
Hayward, California

EDUCATION:
B.A., Chico State University.

PUBLICATIONS:
Books:
Suburbia.
Our Kind of People.
Working: I Do It For The Money.

Magazines:
Newsweek.

When I started Suburbia I remembered the photographic books that I loved the most; the people who documented America in the 30's, the Farm Security Administration: Russell Lee, Walker Evans, Dorothea Lange. I wanted to do a contemporary look at America. I worked very hard to find homes, things and people who represented the whole. I don't know if there is any such thing as a "typical-looking" person, but I looked for people and an environment that you could cast and ship to the Smithsonian.

What I say is my view. Other people in my genre of photography see it differently. All I can say is that I hope that *my* truth has some sort of universality to it. I pursue as hard as I can and try to understand people and life and how crazy and wonderful and depressing and insane it is. It's an incredible country that we live in.

OLIVIA PARKER
Manchester, Massachusettes

Eight years separate ***Pomegranates*** and ***Moon Under, Earth Under*** in time and thought. Both images have left me in that I am always most involved in new work, but they continue to exist as my footprints through a life in photography.

Pomegranates is an homage to the historical still life. It celebrates an object for its essential quality and bears the traditional reference of fruit on the table top, the moment of ripeness implying death and rebirth to come. ***Pomegranates*** is the most traditional picture I have ever made. I enjoyed making it, and it would have been very easy for me to make a lot of similar pictures with specific reference to the history of still life painting. I did not do that, because for me photography is an exploration, and I had to move along.

Moon Under, Earth Under was made in 1987, recently enough to be close in thought to what I am doing now. The most important difference between this picture and ***Pomegranates*** is that in ***Pomegranates*** I was after the essential qualities of a particular object to be photographed and in ***Moon Under, Earth Under*** I was looking for a quality of the whole photograph in which the objects photographed change according to context. Pomegranates stay pomegranates, but in ***Moon Under, Earth Under*** copier and painted images become context for a metal object which I have used in other pictures and will use again. I know what the metal object was originally. It does not matter, because I am not after the quality of the object. In this image it has shifting references because of the context and the way the photographic materials have recorded colored light reflecting from the metal and paper. One moment it is an ancient vertebrae, the next the trunk of a peculiar elephant lurking outside the frame. That is only the first look; it becomes a lot more. I will not be

— continued on page: 135

BORN: Boston, MA, 1941.

EDUCATION:
1963: B.A., Wellesley College, History of Art.

SELECTED ACCOMPLISHMENTS:
Ephemera, 10 original prints, a portfolio.
Lost Objects, 10 original prints, a portfolio.
1978: Fellowship, The Artist's Foundation.
1981: New Works Commission, The Photographic Resource Center.

PUBLICATIONS:
Books:
Signs Of Life.
Under The Looking Glass.
Weighing The Planets.

Magazines:
American Photographer, Camera Arts, Popular Photography, Camera, Photovision, Art News, The Sciences.

EVA RUBINSTEIN
New York, New York

BORN: Buenos Aires, Argentina, 1933.

EDUCATION:
Scripps College.
Theater Department of the University of California.
New School for Social Research, (Lisette Model).
Private workshop with Diane Arbus.

SELECTED ACCOMPLISHMENTS:
Danced and acted on and off Broadway.
Opened and played in original New York company of The Diary of Anne Frank, 1955-1956.
Associate Fellow, Ezra Stiles College, Yale University.
Member of Polish Institute of Arts & Sciences, New York.

PUBLICATIONS:
Books:
Monograph: Eva Rubinstein, 1974 (USA).
Monograph: Eva Rubinstein, 1983 (Italy & Spain).
Persephone (20 Years of Photographs by Eva Rubinstein) (France).
Lodz: Brief Encounters (Poland).

Magazines:
Life, Time, Newsweek, Popular Photography and Annuals, Camera (Swiss), Photo-ovo (Canada), L'Express, Jours de France (Paris), Photo Magazine (Paris).

The elements are simple: a bed, a mirror, a table. Linen — bed linen, table linen. But each one of these particular objects, being so basic, so common, seems to carry an immense history of its own. So much happens in, on, around a bed — birth, love, death.

A table is , or used to be, the center of the life of a family, and tables per se have been a place where food was prepared, then given and shared. They have been altars, they have been places of ritual and even sacrifice. Linen. Clear or rumpled, bed-linen speaks of the "life" of the bed. Table-linen adds to the significance of the use to which the table is, has been, is about to be—put.

In these two images, one from 1972, one from 1986, but printed for the first time only a few months ago (May 1988) there seems to be something misssing, incomplete. The bed has no pillow. The table, no utensils which would tell us what its purpose is or was. No people. Are they expected? Have they been, taken part, left? Will they return? Everything is in a sense both strangely anonymous and profoundly personal. The bed is certainly in a very particular room, house, place—a place which seems to need repairs, care. But it is clean and bright. Is it sterile? Is it sun-drenched and happy? The cloths (two of them) on the table, are much mended and well-worn, but clearly ironed, pressed, folded, cared for. But where are we? A large seeming place—a rug? A stone floor? Is there a breeze from the left? Where are the chairs? If the event has taken place, there is not a trace of it—not a spot of wine, a crumb of bread, an empty plate or cup.

What these places have been are for me, personally, in their actual moment, and in other ways at this moment, is not important or relevant to another who looks at these
—continued on page: 135

VAL TELBERG
Sag Harbor, New York

Invasion. This is representational art; done as a comment on the war — it is a weird comment, since I remember the mood but no longer recall which war it was — Russian Revolution, Chinese Civil War, Japanese War, Vietnam, Korea. . . .

Event is forgotten, but absurdity is not; and as a page in my visual diary it still comes through — even if now it is tinged by nostalgia.

Men Listening. This was done while on a fellowship at Yaddo, a summer in Upstate New York. Symbolism escapes me. As often happens the moods change and the reaction to symbols evolves from original intent to requirements of the moment — growth of the soul . . . aging of the body . . .

Basically, I do not work for perfection: rather I venerate spontaneity . . . the closer to the subconscious, the truer. Technically, I seek to shorten time between fleeting thought and its recording. Considerations of color, composition, balance are as unimportant to me as the color of paper to a poet. I also suspect that art technology, from linseed oil to sharp lenses conflicts with emotional aura which is the essence of art.

BORN: Moscow, Russia, 1910.

EDUCATION:
North China American School, Tungchow, China.
1932: B.A. Wittenberg College, Ohio.
1941-48: Art Student League, New York (Life Member for 10 years).

SELECTED ACCOMPLISHMENTS:
Illustrated Anais Nin's House of Incest, Swallow Press, Chicago.
1970's involved with avant-garde multi-media productions in collaboration with his wife Lelia Katayen.
Yaddo Fellowship.
Huntington Hartford Foundation Fellowship.

PUBLICATIONS:
Books:
Photography: A Fascet of Modern Art, Deren Coke & D.C. DuPont, 1986.
Making Of A Collection, Photographs From Minneapolis Institute of Art, by C. Hartwell, Aperture, 1985.
Photography And Art Interactions Since 1946, Andy Grundberg & Kathleen McCarthy Gauss, 1987.
Who's Who In American Art.

Magazines:
American Photography, Arts, Fortune Magazine, Life Library of Photography, The New York Times, Afterimage, World and I, Photo Metro.

JOYCE TENNESON
Washington, DC

BORN: Weston, Massachusetts, 1945.

EDUCATION:
1962-63: College of Rombas, France.
B.A. Regis College, Boston, Mass.
M.A. George Washington University, Washington, DC.
Ph.D. Union Graduate School, Antioch College, Yellow Springs Ohio.

SELECTED ACCOMPLISHMENTS:
1978-80: Assoc. Professor of Art, Northern Virginia Community College.
1979-83: Instructor, Corcoran School of Art, Washington, DC.
1981-82: Grant, D.C. Commission on the Arts.

PUBLICATIONS:
Books:
In/Sights: Self Portraits by Women, David Godine, Boston, MA.
Joyce Tenneson, Photographs, David Godine, Boston, MA.
Exposures: Photographs by Joyce Tenneson, by Steven Carothers, Boca Museum, Boca Raton, FL, 1988.
Au Dela, Color Photographs by Joyce Tenneson, Contrejour, Paris.

Magazines:
Vogue, "W", New York, American Photographer, Collectors Photography, Zoom, L.A. Style.

Suzanne, 1986. This image seems to speak to almost everyone, though the reasons very much vary. During the past two years it has been the cover for two magazines (one American, the other German). It was chosen as the poster image for an exhibition in Lausanne, Switzerland, and it has been reproduced in magazines around the world over twenty times.

A great deal of my imagery is polarizing; people either like it, or they feel unsettled by it in some way. With this image of ***Suzanne,*** nearly everybody has a strong positive reaction. Some of the reactions I have collected are: "It's mesmerizing and haunting"; "She looks like an Ingres beauty"; "She is mysterious, but not threatening"; "I wouldn't be afraid to meet her—in fact, I'd like to take care of her"; "She looks like she was once in an asylum." And when I took the image to be framed, I was told that it was "a great self-portrait!" I told the framer he had missed the age difference between us only by about 20 years, although since then many people have said the same thing as the framer.

Three Women, Two Men, One Child, 1987. This image provokes intense reactions. One editor said she loved it, but wouldn't reproduce it because it reminded her of a concentration camp scene. Another editor said it reminded him of a bath scene. And I've had about every reaction in between.

The image came into being without any advance previsualization at all. It was the end of a long day of shooting, and I simply asked everyone present to get in front of the camera for a group shot. Because we had had such an intense day, people just seemed to take these positions naturally. I knew it was powerful when I pressed the shutter; it retains that same power for me each time I look at it.

GEORGE TICE
Iselin, New Jersey

Two Amish Boys, Lancaster, Pennsylvania, 1962. This photograph was taken for my first book, Fields of Peace, A Pennsylvania German Album. I met up with the two boys as they were coming down the hill. My contact sheet shows three exposures were made; a close-up of the two looking straight into the camera, a profile of the younger of the two brothers and for the final exposure, I asked them to walk back up the hill.

I still have the first print I made from this negative. It was made expressly for the Vailsburg Camera Club's black and white print competition and it won Print of the Month. The back of the mount has rubber stampings from the various photographic salons it was exhibited in: Baltimore, Rochester, Wichita, Pittsburg, Detroit, Youngstown Photographic Society, California State Fair, Illinois State Fair. I was thrilled that the Illinois State Fair reproduced this photograph in their catalog and disappointed when I read the credit line — Lee Wing Tong (a typo). In all the salons I submitted this photograph to, it was never rejected. I stopped exhibiting in salons in 1966.

As I view that print today it looks as though it was taken by moonlight. It had to be printed dark because the light box the camera club used for competitions would wash-out a normal print. Where I felt the sky was too bright, I toned it down by rubbing black oil paint into the emulsion. To cover-up my handwork a laquer was sprayed over the entire surface.

I first titled it "Companions," but after it was published in The New York Times with the caption, "Two Amish Boys," that became its title. A man from New Jersey wrote to me about buying one after seeing it in the newspaper. That print I made on a tapestry surfaced paper, and instead of signing it on the mount, I stenciled my name thinking that

—continued on page: 135

BORN: Newark, NJ, 1938.

EDUCATION:
Photographer in U.S. Navy from 1956-1959.

SELECTED ACCOMPLISHMENTS:
NEA fellowship.
Guggenheim Fellowship.
Grand Prix du Festival d' Arles.

PUBLICATIONS:
Monographs:
Urban Landscapes, 1975.
George A. Tice/Photographs/ 1953-73, 1975.
Paterson, 1972.
George A. Tice-Photographs, 1953-73, 1975.
Urban Romantic, The Photographs of George Tice, 1982.

Books:
Artie Van Blarcum, 1977.
Fields of Peace. w/Millen Brand, 1970.
Seacoast Maine, w/Martin Dibner, 1973.
Goodbye, River, Goodbye, w/ George Mendoza, 1971.
Lincoln, 1984.
Hometowns, 1988.

JERRY UELSMANN
Gainesville, Florida

I try to begin working with no preconceived ideas. Each click of the shutter suggests an emotional and visual involvement, and contains the potential of establishing greater rapport with some quintessential aspect of the subject and my feelings toward it, both conscious and preconscious. My contact sheets become a kind of visual diary of all the things I have seen and experienced with my camera. They contain the seeds from which my images grow. Before entering the darkroom, I ponder these sheets, seeking fresh and innovative juxtapositions that expand the possibilities of the initial subject matter. The anticipation of discovering these possibilties becomes my greatest joy. Ultimately, my hope is to amaze myself.

BORN: Detroit, Michigan, 1934.

EDUCATION:
1957: B.F.A. Rochester Institute of Technology.
1960: M.S. and M.F.A. from Indiana University, Bloomington.
Studied with Ralph Hattersley, Minor White and Henry Holmes Smith, Beaumont Newhall.

SELECTED ACCOMPLISHMENTS:
Professor at University of Florida, Gainesville since 1960.
1967: Guggenheim Fellowship.

PUBLICATIONS:
Books:
Jerry N. Uelsmann-Silver Meditations, Morgan & Morgan, Inc., Dobbs Ferry, NY, 1975.
The Criticism of Photography as Art: The Photographs of Jerry N. Uelsmann, by John Ward, University of Florida Press, Gainsville, FL, 1970.
Jerry N. Uelsmann, Aperture, Inc., Millerton, NY (Updated 1973) 1970.
Jerry N. Uelsmann, Witkin-Berely, Ltd., Roslyn Heights, NY., (portfolio).
Eight Photographs: Jerry Uelsmann, Doubleday and Company, New York, NY, 1970.
Jerry N. Uelsmann-Photography from 1975-79, Columbia College, Chicago, IL, 1980.
Jerry N. Uelsmann Twenty Five Years: A Retrospective, by James L. Enyeart, New York Graphics Society, Boston, MA 1982.
Uelsmann: Process and Perception, University of Florida Press, Gainsville, FL, 1985, (updated 1988).

TODD WALKER
Tucson, Arizona

Torn Pair, Lithograph Number 169. This print has been widely exhibited. It is representative of the landscape work to which I returned after teaching for several years at the University of Florida. In the seven years I was there I almost forgot about the mountains. My return west renewed my energy to work in this landscape with new insight and intensity. This phase commenced in 1977 and continues.

Untitled, *1969.* It was made as an important part of my mental transition from my role as photographic illustrator. This is a Sabattier effect silver print. Each of such prints is unique due to the nature of this process. I look back on this work with great pride. I moved on from this period with a feeling of accomplishment. The response such work received from Wynn Bullock and others gave me the confidence I then needed to leave the commercial world.

BORN: Salt Lake City, Utah, 1917.

EDUCATION:
1939-41: Art Center School, Los Angeles, CA.
1939-40: Glendale Junior College, CA.

SELECTED ACCOMPLISHMENTS:
Professor, Emeritus, University of Arizona, Tucson.
1983: National Endowment for the Arts Photography Fellowship.
1976: Florida Council for the Arts Photography Fellowship.
1971: National Foundation for the Arts Photography Fellowship.

PUBLICATIONS:
Books:
23 Self Published Books, Portfolios as The Thumbprint Press, including:
Twentyseven Photographs, The Thumbprint Press, 1974.
Three Soliloquies, The Thumbprint Press, 1977.
See, The Thumbprint Press, 1976.
Untitled 38, 1985, Friends of Photography, 35 color reproductions.

Magazines:
U.S. Camera, PSA Journal, Applied Photography, Artweek, The Village Voice, The New York Times, Creative Camera, Afterimage, Modern Photography, American Photographer.

JACK WELPOTT
San Francisco, California

BORN: Kansas City, Kansas, 1923.

EDUCATION:
B.S. Indiana University.
M.S. Indiana University.
M.F.A. Indiana University.

SELECTED ACCOMPLISHMENTS:
1979: National Endowment for the Arts.
1983: Polaroid Corporation/work with the 20 x 24 camera.
(31) One Man Shows given between 1981 and 1988.

PUBLICATIONS:
Books:
The Halide Conversion, Min Gallery, Tokyo, 1988.
Master Photographs, International Center of Photography, 1988.
Das Aktfoto, Muncher Stadtmuseum, 1985.
The Naked and the Nude, Jorge Lewinski, London, 1987.
Le Nu Dans La Photographie, 1840-1986, Germany 1987.
La Photographie Creative, Bibliotheque National.
Faces, History of the Portrait, NY Graphics Society, NY.
Women and Other Visions, Morgan and Morgan.
The Print, Time Life Books.

My most popular photograph is titled ***Sabine.*** The photograph was made in Arles, France, in 1973, in what was at the time, Jerry Uelsmann's bedroom. Jerry and I were doing a workshop along with Judy Dater and Lee Friedlander. It was a hot summer and the models for the workshop liked to hang out in the little house we were living in, and being models, they preferred to be semi-nude. This provided a wonderful week of doing figure photography and I spent much time photographing Sabine — she reminded me of my mother. While she remained cool, I sweated over a hot Bronica. I almost didn't print the picture because, at first, I thought I had failed. It has since become a favorite for many people and has been widely published. I have a number of others of Sabine that I think are as good. Perhaps someday I will publish a portfolio.

The second picture is called ***65 Ave. D'la Bourdonnais, Paris,*** and was done in 1985. It is looking into Benedict Fernandez's bedroom. He was away at the time chasing rats through the sewers of Paris (that's what he likes to photograph). Benedict, Brooke Gray and I were living in that apartment while doing a workshop in Paris. I like the photograph because it is so complex. It is, as the French would say, a tour de force. I am looking into four rooms at one time and I would like to believe it is loaded with symbolism.

COLE WESTON
Carmel, California

BORN: Los Angeles, CA, 1919.

EDUCATION:
1937: Cornish School in Seattle, Washington for three years, graduated in Theater Arts.

SELECTED ACCOMPLISHMENTS:
1966: Served three years as Sunset Center Cultural Director for the City of Carmel.
1973: Spent eight months sailing the "Scaldis" to the South Seas, doing a film on how a man can take his family and "Escape to Reality".
Director, Forest Theater Guild, 40 yrs. Plays such as: "Of Mice and Men", "Our Town", "Winterset", "Oliver", "Camelot", "Pipe Dream", "View From the Bridge", "Summer and Smoke".

PUBLICATIONS:
Books:
His work has been published in:
Not Man Apart, Sierra Club.
The Sea Around Us, by Rachael Carson.
Cole Weston: Eighteen Photographs.
Record Album Cover: Le Men.

Magazines:
Life, Look, Holiday, Readers Digest, Popular Photography.

EDWARD WESTON

BORN: Highland Park, Illinois, 1886.
DIED: Carmel, California, 1958.

EDUCATION:
1908-1911: Illinois College of Photography.

SELECTED ACCOMPLISHMENTS:
1917: Elected to the London Salon.
1932: Formed Group f.64 with Ansel Adams and Willard Van Dyke.
1937: First photographer to receive a Guggenheim Fellowship.
1938: Guggenheim Fellowship extended.
1948: Was the subject of the motion picture, The Photographer.

PUBLICATIONS:
Books:
Edward Weston: Nudes, notes by Charis Wilson, 1977.
Edward Weston: Fifty Years, Ben Maddow, 1973.
The Daybooks, vol. 2: California 1927-34, intro. by Nancy Newhall, 1966, vol. 1: Mexico, intro. by Beaumont Newhall, foreward & note by Nancy Newhall, 1961, vols. 1 & 2 repr. 1971.
Fifty Photographs: Edward Weston, designed & ed. by Merle Armitage, 1947.
The Photographs of Edward Weston, Nancy Newhall, 1946.
California and The West, Charis Wilson, 1940, rev. ed., 1978.
Seeing California with Edward Weston, 1939.
The Art of Edward Weston, designed & ed. by Merle Armitage, 1932.

STATEMENTS CONTINUED:

BRUCE BARNBAUM
—continued from page 104.

ation to location, one friend, Vince Buck, kept pulling out travel and advertising brochures extolling the wonders each place had to offer. We kidded him unmercifully about the junk that he kept pushing at us. On New Year's Eve we arrived in Page, Arizona, where he again rummaged through his stack of brochures. He came across three items that all seemed to be referring to the same narrow canyon, but each gave it a different name, so we weren't sure if it was one, two, or three places. One called it "the maze," another "the labyrinth," and the third, "the corkscrew." Each one, however, located it in "Antelope Wash."

It sounded interesting enough that we sought it out the next day. We found Antelope Wash and several stretches of low, twisting, narrow canyons within it. They were fascinating, and I photographed for hours in them, but Vince kept insisting that the area referred to was farther up the wash. By late afternoon, I reluctantly acceded to his demands to look farther, and we jumped into my 4-wheel drive to investigate some more. He was right! Another mile up, the wash was blocked by a sandstone wall—a dike—that prevented further automobile travel. But there was a crack in the dike that we entered. It was like stepping into another universe! I have never experienced anything like that before or since. We walked up this narrow, convoluted, sensuous world, with our mouths agape, staring upward into the infinity of surrealistic forms. I immediately saw a photograph, but I had left my camera with the others when Vince and I went up the wash in the late afternoon. That was January 1, 1980, and all I could think was, "What a way to start a new decade!"

The next morning I went directly back to Antelope Canyon, and set up my camera on "Circular Chimney" as my first image. I only needed to refine my camera position from my vision of it the previous afternoon to make the image a reality.

To me Antelope Canyon is cosmic. I see forms in it that strike me as force fields between cosmic objects — as if I could see the forces between objects instead of the objects themselves. To me, its walls are part of the field; they do not define the limits of the field as walls define the limits of spaces in the normal sense. ***Circular Chimney, Antelope Canyon,*** started my photography of slit canyons, which has become an ongoing project. I feel that it is my most significant photograph for its uniqueness and for the new direction that it gave me.

PAUL CAPONIGRO
— continued from page 106.

something came from the photograph and simultaneously welled up from within me. The photograph simply said, "Teachings from the ancient fathers!" — This phrase stuck in my mind and was to be recalled and repeated by me over the next several weeks in an effort to understand what it meant; this image of stone was haunting me.

The passage of time and concern with other matters eroded the urgency of seeking the answer to that enigmatic utterance from a silvered surface. Seven years later I was awarded a Guggenheim Fellowship which brought me to Ireland, where I encountered the prehistoric megaliths. The megaliths are ordered groups of man placed stones which are potent with mystery and meaning. I spent years photographing these ancient stone monuments in an effort to comprehend the message which was written in their undisturbed silence. At some point while photographing these stones I realized that the meaning of the phrases, "Teachings from the ancient fathers," as given by the ***Rock Wall*** print, could be found here. The stone of ***Rock Wall*** met the stone of the ancient monuments as I unwittingly entered a timeless moment of communion with this material. Only in recent years has it come to light that there is a sophistication of knowledge expressed through the uniqueness of these monuments . . . knowledge which could teach us today.

New York City, 1964. "One time while photographing a still life of fruits, my eye gravitated to the attractive shape of the single red delicious apple in the bowl, and I decided to use it as my subject. As my attention was caught by the simplicity and beauty of this apple, rational thoughts about the manipulation of materials were suspended; instead, I dwelled only on its form and the light that was reflecting from it. Something was impressing me about this apple, but I avoided attempts at defining it. It was not until much later, when I printed the negative, that I realized what I had responded to. The first few prints I pulled simply stated the subject as beautiful apple, and though it was pleasing, it seemed to lack the deeper impression I had experienced while making the negative. Something urged me to print it deeper in tone, and when I saw the new print, I was thrilled with its impact. The darker print allowed the surface reflections of the apple to shine forth as points of light, and I was amazed to see, not a rendition of an apple, but a galaxy of stars. I reflected on why I had not seen that exact potential in the apple when I first photographed it and realized that I was receiving the message on a deeper, subconscious level. In looking back at earlier successful photographs, I recalled the same meditative stance had attended the process of making those images."

JUDY DATER
— continued from page 107.

without the glass in front of it. The glass was like a film over the eyes. The idea came to me to do a self-portrait with my hands seeming to be pulling away the glass (film) from the landscape so that one might see more clearly. It was a metaphor for me in regard to my own life, my personal quest to see things more clearly. It was the first in a series of self-portraits which continued through 1984.

TOM McCARTNEY
— continued from page 116

with it the weather and light that is perfect for photography. This particular day was spent in the Blue Hill region. A sagging porch with white pickets, an aging store front and an old opera house proved to be worthy subjects, but there was a feeling that my efforts were misspent. The late afternoon produced a slight but not unexpected chill, and I decided to call the day uneventful and travel northwards to the town of Castine and enjoy the comforts of the Castine Inn.

The road followed closely along the tidal marsh of Penobscot Bay and in a nearby tidal slough I noticed two boats gently being nudged by the incoming tide. The relationship of the boats, their shadows, the mud flat and grassy banks produced the necessary lines, shapes, textures and perspective needed for an expressive photograph. The atmosphere and mood was one of quietude and peacefulness, and this was the emotion I wished to convey. The subject brightness range required a normal exposure and development time in order for the negative to produce a tonal range consisting primarily of soft and subtle middle values that would allow the print to suggest the serenity of a Maine afternoon.

OLIVIA PARKER
— continued from page 124.

more specific in words, because that can limit a viewer's possibilities of exploring an image visually in the way paraphrasing a poem gets in the way of a deep reading.

The approach to ***Moon Under, Earth Under*** remains interesting to me because it has infinite possibilities for exploring the potential richness of arranged photographs. I find nothing wrong with creating a picture which seduces the eye, but to remain interesting to me an image must have its own complexity of meaning beyond the surface.

EVA RUBINSTEIN:
— continued from page 125.

images. Each will see/read/feel through his and her own experience, vision, dream. Or perhaps, will see nothing at all. I turn my back on a rumpled bed in order to make an image of its reflection in a mirror — "reflections" on a bed? (Hadn't thought of that at all until eleven years later, in 1983 walking—talking through an exhibit of mine with some students—at their request)

I face the table but not quite "squarely" — I am above it! Looking down— and so on, and on, probably. I hope. ***The Bed in the Mirror*** has been in print often since its birth in 1972. It seems to be viable, is expected to live. ***The Clothed Table*** is something of a new-born. Time will tell if it is strong enough internally to survive and become one of the chosen few.

GEORGE TICE
— continued from page 128

more artistic in my misguided effort to be considered an artist. It was the first print I ever sold. In the meantime of 25 years I've sold many prints of this my most popular photograph. Mostly 8x10's, some 11x14's, and a few 16x20's. My guess is I've printed this negative on perhaps fifty occasions. Recent prints show a much softer, full-scaled interpretation. The square 2 1/4x 2 1/4 negative is cropped verticle; lately I added a second chimney to the right edge. It keeps changing.

As my most often published photograph it has proven to be an inspiration to some. I've starting collecting Two Amish Boys in other mediums. So far, I have two pen and ink drawings; one is a postcard; the other an illustration for a cookbook. A third piece is in marquetry and is made of many different kinds of wood. I should have started collecting sooner as I've seen others and heard of more.

Charley and Violet on Their Houseboat, Jersey City, New Jersey, *1979.* Upon the recommendation of John Szarkowski, (Director of Photography, MOMA) I received a commission from an architectural firm in Princeton, New Jersey to photograph Liberty Park. My photographs were to depict the derelict site as it existed before transformation into New Jersey's big urban park. The uniqueness of the site is the magnificent views of Manhattan, Ellis Island, and the Statue of Liberty. The architect's plans, scale models and my photographs were exhibited the following month at the Museum of Modern Art's Department of Architecture.

For the photograph of Charlie and Violet their appearance was unplanned. I didn't know who lived there. I composed a photograph of their houseboat without them. Carefully I included Ellis Island into the ground glass and by lining-up the smokestack with the skyline I tied the composition together. One exposure was made in this manner when a car pulled up and Charlie and Violet stepped into my frame exclaiming, "Well, take our picture!"

A few days later I returned with a print for them. They seemed pleased; they said were going to buy a frame and hang it inside. I never saw them again.

SELECTED COLLECTIONS:

BRUCE BARNBAUM
Amon Carter Museum, Ft. Worth, TX.
Detroit Institute of Art, MI.
International Center for Photography, New York, NY.
Los Angeles County Museum of Art.
New Orleans Museum of Art.
Preus Museum of Photography, Horten, Norway.

JUDY DATER
Center for Creative Photography, University of Arizona, Tucson, AZ.
Fogg Art Museum, Harvard University, Boston, MA.
High Art Museum, Atlanta, GA.
International Center for Photography, New York, NY.
International Museum of Photography, Rochester, NY.
Metropolitan Museum of Art, New York, NY.
MOMA, San Francisco, CA.
MOMA, New York, NY.

ANDREAS FEININGER
The Museum of Modern Art, New York, NY.
International Museum of Photography at George Eastman House Rochester, NY.
The Metropolitan Museum of Art, New York, NY.
Victoria and Albert Museum, London, England.
San Francisco Museum of Modern Art, San Fransisco, CA.
Feininger's Archive is on deposit with the Center for Creative Photography, University of Arizona, Tucson, AZ.

SANDI FELLMAN
Museum of Modern Art, New York, NY.
The Metropolitan Museum of Art, New York, NY.
Minneapolis Institute of Art, Minneapolis, MN.
Bibliotheque Nationale, Paris, France.
Polaroid International Collection, Offenbach, Germany.
Museum of Fine Arts, Houston, TX.

ROBERT FICHTER
California Museum of Photography, Riverside, CA.
Center for Creative Photography, Univ. of Arizona, Tempe, AZ.
Madison Art Center, Madison, WI.
Los Angeles County Museum, Los Angeles, CA.
University of Colorado, Boulder, CO.
National Gallery, Washington, D.C.

RALPH GIBSON
Museum of Modern Art, New York, NY.
Bibliotheque National, Paris, France.
International Museum of Photography at George Eastman House, Rochester, NY.
Fogg Art Museum, Boston, MA.
Metropolitan Museum of Art, New York, NY.
Center for Creative Photography, Tucson, AZ.

LES KRIMS
George Eastman House, Rochester, NY.
The Museum of Modern Art, New York, NY.
Bibliotheque Nationale, Paris France.
San Francisco Museum of Modern Art, San Francisco, CA.
Boston Museum of Fine Arts, Boston, MA.

SALLY MANN
The Metropolitan Museum of Art, New York, NY.
Museum of Modern Art, New York, NY.
The National Museum of American Art, Washington, DC.
Corcoran Gallery of Art, Washington, DC.
Hirshhorn Museum, Washington, DC.
San Francisco Museum of Art, San Fransisco, CA.

TOM McCARTNEY
Metropolitan Museum of Art, New York, NY.
Milwaukee Art Museum, Milwaukee, WI.
Norton Gallery of Art, West Palm Beach, FL.
University of Northern Iowa, Cedar Falls, IA.
Rochester Institute of Technology, Rochester, New York, NY.
Santa Barbara Museum of Art, Santa Barbara, CA.

SHEILA METZNER
The Metropolitan Museum of Art, New York, NY.
The Museum of Modern Art, New York, NY.
Chrysler Museum, Norfolk, VA.
Saks Fifth Avenue, New York NY.
International Center for Photography, New York, NY.
Polaroid Corp., Boston, MA.

JOEL MEYEROWITZ
Boston Museum of Fine Arts, Boston, MA.
Museum of Modern Art, New York, NY.
Philadelphia Museum of Art, Philadelphia, PA.
St. Louis Art Museum, St. Louis, MO.
Virginia Museum of Fine Arts, Richmond, VA.
Chicago Art Institute, Chigago, IL.

DUANE MICHALS
Museum of Modern Art, New York, NY.

International Museum of Photography, George Eastman House Rochester, NY.
Smithsonian Institution, Washington, DC.
The Metropolitan Museum of Art, New York, NY.
Musee d'Art Moderne de la Ville de Paris, France.
Philadelphia Museum of Art, Philadelphia, PA.

BEA NETTLES
Museum of Modern Art, New York, NY.
National Museum of American Art, Smithsonian Inst., Washington, DC.
Metropolitan Museum of Art, New York, NY.
Center for Creative Photography, Tucson, AZ.
Polaroid International Collection, Offenbach, Germany.

BEAUMONT NEWHALL
Center For Creative Photography, University of Arizona, AZ.
International Center of Photography, New York, NY.
Houston Museum of Fine Arts, Houston, TX.
Fogg Art Museum, Harvard University, Cambridge, MA.
Australian National Gallery, Caneberra, Australia.
Sante Fe Museum of Fine Arts, NM.

ARNOLD NEWMAN
Metropolitan Museum of Art, New York, NY.
Museum of Modern Art, New York, NY.
Chicago Art Institute, Chicago, IL.
Philadelphia Museum of Art, Philadelphia, PA.
Center for Creative Photography, University of Arizona.
Victoria and Albert Museum, London, England.
Stedeligk Museum, Amsterdam, The Netherlands.
Israel Museum, Jerusalem, Israel.
Tel Aviv Museum, Tel Aviv, Israel.
Australia National Gallery, Canberra, Australia.

OLIVIA PARKER
The Art Institute of Chicago, Chicago, IL.
The Museum of Modern Art, New York, NY.
National Museum of Australia, Canberra, Australia.
International Museum of Photography at George Eastman House Rochester, NY.
The Boston Museum of Fine Arts, Boston, MA.
The Victoria and Albert Museum, London, England.

EVA RUBINSTEIN
The Metropolitan Museum of Art, New York, NY.
The International Center of Photography, New York, NY.
Bibliotheque Nationale, Paris, France.
The Israel Museum, Israel.
Musee d'Art Moderne de la Ville de Paris, France.
Fondation Van Gogh, Arles, France.
The Imaginary Museum, Cologne, Germany.
The Museum of Modern Art (Muzeum Sztuki) Lodz, Poland.

VAL TELBERG
Brooklyn Museum, New York, NY.
The Museum of Modern Art, New York, NY.
New Orleans Museum of Art, New Orleans, LA.
Princeton University Art Museum, Princeton, NJ.
San Francisco Museum of Modern Art, San Fransisco, CA.
Smithsonian Institution, Washington, DC.
Getty Museum, Malibu, CA.
Metropolitan Museum, New York, NY.
Santa Barbara Museum of Art, Santa Barbara, CA.

JOYCE TENNESON
Boca Raton Museum of Art, Boca Raton, FL.
Library of Congress, Washington, DC.
Smithsonian Institute, Washington, DC.
Bibliotheque Nationale, Paris, France.
Corcoran Gallery of Art, Washington, DC.
Rufino Tamayo Museum of Contemporary Art, Mexico.
City of Paris Collection, France.

GEORGE TICE
Art Institute of Chicago, Chicago, IL.
Metropolitan Museum of Art, New York, NY.
Museum of Modern Art, New York, NY.
Bibliotheque Nationale, Paris, France.
Victoria & Albert Museum, London, England.

JERRY UELSMANN
Boca Raton Museum of Art, Boca Raton, FL.
Center for Creative Photography, Tucson, AZ
National Gallery of Australia, Melbourne, Australia.
Musee Reattu, Arles, France.
Museum of Modern Art, New York, NY.
Smithsonian Institute, Washington, DC.
National Gallery of Canada, Ottowa, Ontario, Canada.
National Museum of American Art, Washington, DC.
George Eastman House, Rochester, NY.
Modern Museet, Stockholm, Sweden.
Victoria and Albert Museum, London, England.
The National Museum of Modern Art, Kyoto, Japan.
The Philadelphia Museum of Art, Philadelphia, PA.
San Fransisco Museum of Modern Art, San Fransisco, CA.

TODD WALKER
George Eastman House, Rochester, NY.
Museum of Modern Art, New York, NY.
Center for Creative Photography, Tucson, AZ.
Bibliotheque Nationale, Paris, France.
Philadelphia Museum of Art, Philadelphia, PA.
Chicago Art Institute, Chicago, IL.
National Museum of Modern Art, Kyoto, Japan.

JACK WELPOTT
San Fransisco Museum of Modern Art, San Fransisco, CA.
Bibliotheque National, Paris, France.
Museum of Modern Art, New York, NY.
Center for Creative Photography, Tucson, AZ.
Oakland Museum of Art, Oakland, CA.
George Eastman House, Rochester, NY.
Indiana University, Bloomington, IN.

COLE WESTON
Center for Creative Photography
Private Collections

FOOTNOTES TO ELEMENTS OF ACCEPTANCE:

1. **Dater, Judy,** Artist Statement, 1988.
2. Ibid
3. **Mark, Mary Ellen.** Artist Statement, 1988.
4. **Michals, Duane.** Artist Statement, 1988.
5. **Gibson, Ralph.** Artist Statement, 1988.
6. **Uelsmann, Jerry.** Artist Statement, 1988.
7. **Tenneson, Joyce.** Artist Statement, 1988.
8. **Gibson, Ralph.** Interview by Steven Carothers & Gail Roberts, Nov. 1988.
9. Ibid.
10. **Roger Selby.** Interview by Steven Carothers, 1989.
11. **Mark, Mary Ellen.** Interview by Steven Carothers & Gail Roberts, Nov. 1988.
12. **Michals, Duane.** interview by Steven Carothers & Gail Roberts, Nov. 1988.
13. **Freud, Sigmund.** Creative Writers and Day-Dreaming, edited by James Strachey. (London, 1959).p. 146.

BIBLIOGRAPHY

Arieti, Silvano. Creativity: The Magic Synthesis. New York: Basic Books, Inc., 1976.

Arnheim, Rudolph. Art And Visual Perception. Revised Edition. Berkeley, CA: University of California Press., 1974.

Browne, Turner and Partnow, Elaine. Macmillan Biographical Encyclopedia of Photographic Artists & Innovators. New York: Macmillan Publishing Company, 1983.

Henri, Robert. The Art Spirit. New York: J.B. Lippencott Co., 1960.

Hill, Paul and Cooper, Thomas. Dialogue With Photography. New York: Farrar/Straus/Giroux., 1979.

Kandinsky, Wassily. Concerning The Spiritual In Art. New York: Dover Publications, Inc., 1977.

Kennick, W.E. Art And Philosophy: Readings In Aesthetics. New York: St. Martin's Press., 1979.

Szarkowski, John. Looking At Photographs. Boston: Little, Brown And Company., 1988.

PHOTOGRAPH CREDITS & COPYRIGHTS:

Basin Mountain, Approaching Storm — 1973 © Bruce Barnbaum
Circular Chimney, Antelope Canyon — 1980 © Bruce Barnbaum
In The Box — 1962 © Ruth Bernhard
Creation — 1936 © Ruth Bernhard
New York City — 1964 © Paul Caponigro
Rock Wall, Connecticut — 1958 © Paul Caponigro
Imogen & Twinka at Yosemite — 1974 © Judy Dater
My Hands, Death Valley — 1980 © Judy Dater
Moscow — 1959 © Elliott Erwitt, From Personal Exposures, W.W. Norton & Co, 1988.
California — 1955 © Elliott Erwitt, From Personal Exposures, W.W. Norton & Co, 1988.
The Photojournalist — 1951 by Andreas Feininger, Life Magazine, © Time Inc.
Broken Shell — 1971 © Andreas Feininger
Dragon Lady — 1982 © Sandi Fellman
Untitled — 1988 (Fan Piece) © Sandi Fellman
Standard Still-life With Japanese Prints — 1982 © Robert Fichter
Turkey Puzzle — © Robert Fichter
Leda — 1974 © Ralph Gibson
Priest (From Quadrants) — 1975 © Ralph Gibson
Mary's Middle Class — 1985 © Les Krims
Carla Lavorchik — 1988 © Les Krims
Untitled — 1979 (Arm & Wall) © Sally Mann
Jessie at Six — 1988 © Sally Mann
Tiny, In Seattle — 1983 © Mary Ellen Mark
Damm Family in Car, Los Angeles — 1987 © Mary Ellen Mark
Mount McKinley, Alaska — 1982 © Thomas L. McCartney
Eventide, Maine — 1983 © Thomas L. McCartney
Joko Passion — 1985 © Sheila Metzner
Stella, Moulle Shapes — 1986 © Sheila Metzner
Hardwig House — 1976 © Joel Meyerowitz
The Chateau — 1976 © Joel Meyerowitz
All Things Mellow in the Mind — 1987 © Duane Michals (c/o Sidney Janis Gallery)
Illuminated Man — 1968 © Duane Michals (c/o Sidney Janis Gallery)
Feminine/Masculine — 1987 From Life's Lessons © Bea Nettles, 1987
Gavin with the World — 1987 from Life's Lessons © Bea Nettles, 1987
Henri Cartier-Bresson — 1946 © Beaumont Newhall
Mantlepiece, Schloss Leopoldskron, Salzburg, Austria — 1959 © Beaumont Newhall
Picasso — 1954 © Arnold Newman
Sir John Gielgud and Sir Ralph Richardson, London, England — 1978 © Arnold Newman
Reagan on TV — 1970 © William Owens
Companions of the Forest of America — 1974 © William Owens
Pomegranates — 1979 © Olivia Parker
Moon Under, Earth Under — 1987 © Olivia Parker
Bed In Mirror, Rhode Island — 1972 © Eva Rubinstein
Table With Clothe, Arles — 1986 © Eva Rubinstein, 1988
Men Listening — 1962 © Val Telberg (c/o Lawrence Miller Gallery)
Invasion — c. 1954 © Val Telberg (c/o Lawrence Miller Gallery)
Suzanne — 1986 © Joyce Tenneson
3 Women, 2 Men, 1 Child — 1987 © Joyce Tenneson
Two Amish Boys, Lancaster, PA — 1962 George Tice © Fields of Peace
Charlie and Violet on Their Houseboat, Jersey City, NJ — 1979 George Tice © Urban Romantic
Untitled — 1976 [man/library] © Jerry Uelsmann
Untitled — 1981 [rope] © Jerry Uelsmann
Lithograph Number 169 — 1981 © Todd Walker
Untitled — 1969 © Todd Walker